SOTHIS PRESS

Sothis Press aims to completely reimagine the public domain book with an emphasis on universal access to captivatingly designed print editions. We believe that technology will enable every single book ever published to be perpetually accessible in beautiful print form. Sothis is beauty in ubiquity.

www.sothis.press
1 Waterhouse Square, London, ECIN 2ST

Motion Study for the Handicapped

Frank B. Gilbreth

SOTHIS PRESS

ISBN 978-1-0368-0001-7

Motion Study for the Handicapped
is in the public domain.

This edition is published by
Sothis Press The company
is registered in England and Wales.
The Company Number is 14900389.

MOTION STUDY FOR THE HANDICAPPED

BY

FRANK B. GILBRETH

Major, Engineers, R.C. (honourably discharged), Consulting Management Engineer, Member Franklin Institute, American Society of Mechanical Engineers, Past Vice-President Society for the Promotion of Engineering Education

Author of "Fatigue Study," "Applied Motion Study"

AND

LILLIAN MOLLER GILBRETH, PH.D.

LONDON

GEORGE ROUTLEDGE & SONS, LTD.

BROADWAY HOUSE, 68-74, CARTER LANE, E.C.

1920

PREFACE

BY

COLONEL W. O. OWEN

IN writing this preface it comes back to my mind that the first thing I ever heard Frank B. Gilbreth talk about was the value of the study of the crippled by the motion picture camera. This, however, is only one small part of the very important subject, the study of motion in animals and machinery by means of that very important, if new, method, namely: the moving picture with time and distance showing their relations the one to the other in each succeeding picture. This by having the entire background of the picture sub-divided into four-inch squares, thus giving a measure of distance in every part of the field, and when a continuous torque clock is also taken as a part of the picture it adds the element of time in relation to each picture. This picture of the running clock enables one to have the exact motion, time and all, reproduced by making the clock on the screen and the actual clock keep pace the one with the other. It also enables one to produce a simultaneous motion chart. Thus it was that Gilbreth laid the facts themselves before the medical men—the biological engineers.

At the beginning of the war I was instructed by the then Surgeon-General of the Army (Major-General William C. Gorgas) to establish a Section of Graphics in the Army Medical Museum, which was to include drawings in black and white, in color, paintings, sculpture, photographs, moving pictures, etc. In studying these questions one of the first names that came before me was that of Frank B. Gilbreth, of Providence, Rhode Island. I at once wrote to him, telling him my troubles and asking for assistance. His answer came promptly: he, himself, coming, bringing one of his assistants with him and all of the material necessary to show me the details of how the matter was to be accomplished. Meanwhile, I had been talking with the Officers of the War College, Colonel Bowman, Majors Ellis and E. B. Garey. They were having troubles of their own, but I, having seen what Gilbreth had in mind, thought that his knowledge of the subject would make him of far greater value to the United States on duty with the War College than it could be in the Surgeon-General's Office in the Army Medical Museum. I told Colonel Bowman of Gilbreth. I brought the two together, and as a result, Gilbreth, who had already been commissioned as Major of Engineers, was detailed to the General Staff, and sent to Fort Sill, Oklahoma, to study the methods for standardizing the training of soldiers. There were many important studies made before he became seriously ill with pneumonia which was followed by rheumatism, which disabled him and compelled him to return to Walter Reed Hospital in this City.

One of the most interesting experiences of my life was to go to this Hospital and see this man bedridden, utterly unable to move any single joint in his entire body without pain, scarcely able to move at all, his mind working all the time with some new problem, questioning me concerning my work, making suggestions as to better methods, always something new and better than I was doing. The last thing on earth in his mind was his own physical condition. Just so soon as the authorities of the Hospital would permit him to hobble out on crutches, down he came to spend the day in the Instruction Laboratory, always helping, always cheery. Never will I forget his SIMULTANEOUS MOTION CHARTS or his TIME AND DISTANCE MOTION PICTURES, nor shall I soon lose my memories of his explanations of the ANIMATED DIAGRAM as a new method of writing out one's idea of what takes place in an optical apparatus, in an electrical machine and other machines.

It was these ideas of his that gave me the design that enabled me to make the success that was made of the Instruction Laboratory, for they enabled me when Louis B. Wilson, of the Mayo Foundation, joined this force, to accept his ideas and ideals, and enabled him to gather the material which will in the near future, I hope, give this Army Medical Museum a great name.

The TIME AND DISTANCE MOVING PICTURE and the ANIMATED DIAGRAM are the two outstanding new methods of STUDY AND TEACHING. They are both world propositions, and the country which first realizes this fact and makes these two methods a part of their national life, not only for their handicapped but for their school children in the primary schools, in the secondary schools, and in the post graduate schools, will be the country that will be the best prepared in that center of all things human, for *it will be the center of human intelligence*—far better than being the center of banking, merchandize, or any other single thing, for it embraces them all.

No Nation can do anything which will so advance its people as to furnish them with standard methods, ever improving their ONE BEST WAY.

W. O. OWEN,
COLONEL, UNITED STATES ARMY (retired).

Washington, D.C., 3rd July, 1919.

CONTENTS

INTRODUCTION

THE aim of this book is to present methods of least waste in training and placing the handicapped, to tell not only what has been done and what can be done but also actually *how* to do it and *why* it should be done in this manner.

Progress demands coöperation. It implies that all those interested in an activity shall put their information at each other's disposal. It is for this reason that the Motion Study method of handling the handicapped problem is here presented. The papers included were presented before groups interested in the crippled soldier problem from different aspects—before engineers, educators, manufacturers, medical men, nurses, and philanthropists. An endeavor was made in each case not only to adapt the method to the need of a particular group but also to outline the fundamentals in such a manner as to insure each group coöperating with the others interested.

Dealing as it does with the individual possibilities of each worker and with every type of work as an adequate opportunity for some individual, Motion Study naturally presented itself as an available, adequate and universally applicable method for solving the problems of the handicapped.

It was in the early days of August 1914, while we were standing in front of one of the bulletin boards of the newspapers of our city reading the War bulletins, that we realized what a tremendous problem this would be, covering men of all nationalities and training; covering every step in the process of reconstruction, from cheering the wounded to replacing the re-educated; involving and enlisting sympathetic coöperation of every member of the community and especially of the handicapped, and depending for its success upon unification of efforts and widespread education as to needs.

We realized that the immediate necessity was for a change in methods of education. Our long experience had brought to our attention most forcibly the fact that the usual way of doing work is much less efficient than the One Best Way. We knew that the practice of this One Best Way will enable the worker without difficulty to become three or more times as efficient in his trade as he has been before its use. Supplemented by a proper functionalization of the work, we realized that this teaching and practice of the One Best Way could enable us to train the handicapped workers either to return to their old trades or to undertake new lines of work successfully.

Being thus convinced, and having our knowledge of conditions in this country reinforced by personal observations made since the outbreak of the European War in Italy, Switzerland, Germany, Denmark, Sweden, Holland, France and England, we deemed it advisable to go to Washington the morning that War was declared by this country. Immediately upon arrival we called upon Dr. Martin and Dr. Simpson of the Council of National Defense and explained to them the great need of Motion Study for the crippled who would sooner or later come back into the industries. At their suggestion we called upon Surgeon-General Gorgas. After two interviews that enabled us to explain our project thoroly and to show him the various pictures that we had already made of our studies, General Gorgas appointed us, shortly, members of a committee, the other members of which were famous surgeons, which committee made definite recommendations to the Surgeon-General for the re-education of the crippled soldiers.

The splendid development of the work of the Surgeon-General's Department for the handicapped need not be dwelt upon here. We have had the pleasure of coöperating most closely with the Motion Study Laboratory placed by General Gorgas under the most able guidance of Colonel William O. Owen, and of working with him during the period of selecting and installing the devices and methods of his very efficient laboratory. Supplementing this experience on the laboratory side, was a prolonged experience in the hospital and recuperation centers themselves, with ample time to watch recoveries of hundreds of soldiers and to see the progress in re-education in the wards and workshops.

Thru the invitation of Lieutenant-Colonel Bordley and in coöperation with Mr. A. B. Segur, the able director of the Red Cross Institute for the Blind in Baltimore which is operating under the Surgeon-General's Department, we have coöperated in the application of Motion Study methods to the re-education of the blinded and have visited training centers in this country and in England for the purpose of studying the methods in use and of assisting in adapting them to a closer relationship to the training of all handicapped, and to the industrial needs of our country.

Our ultimate findings in all these investigations for the handicapped confirm our original theories as to the methods to be used. These should be similar for all handicapped,—soldiers and civilians alike. They apply equally well to the maimed and the blinded. They involve determining the One Best Way to do work and teaching it thru the most efficient learning process. The expense incurred is warranted because of the triple return:—first, in the economic results of enabling the handicapped to become efficient producers; second, in the educational results from having the handicapped act as examples to normal producers, and third, in that durable satisfaction that comes from enabling a number of disheartened men not only to make good against heavy odds but in many cases to date their progress from the time they were handicapped.

The War has brought many remarkable changes. None perhaps will have more far-reaching beneficial effect than the change in attitude toward the handicapped, indicated by the universal use of the word "handicapped" today instead of the "crippled" of the before-the-War period. Only those who have been handicapped or who have worked intimately with them for years can realize what this means. They have become a recognized part of the industrial community,—welcomed and admired, an element that stands for both progress and maintenance. They stand increasingly as exponents of Motion Study and of Fatigue Study; as successful specialists; as unsurpassed coöperators.

It is impossible to mention by name all who have assisted in our work. We desire to express our appreciation of coöperation of the following:—

Prof. Jules Amar
Prof. W. S. Ayars
Mr E. E. Barney
Mr George Edward Barton
Mr Russell Bond
Dr J. G. Bunker
Mr James F. Butterworth
Dr M. Canavan
Prof. A. F. Stanley Kent
Mr Douglas McMurtie
Mr W. W. Macon
Dr F. L. Marshall
Mr Fred J. Miller
Col. W. O. Owen
Sir Arthur Pearson, Bart.
Mr V. S. Petterson
Mr E. R. Pike
Mr Calvin Rice

Dean A. Cullamore
Mr George.W Dickerman
Dr W. R. Dunton, Jr.
Mr Eugene Eichel
Mr Chas. de Freminville
Dr H. E. Hosley
Mr George Iles
Mr Waldemar Kaempffert
Capt. Frank C. Sanborn
Prof. George Schlesinger
Mr A. B. Segur
Dr E. E. Southard
Prof. Henry J. Spooner
Mr Bradley Stoughton
Mr C. N. Underwood
Prof. Volmer
Prof. L. W. Wallace

Along with these the many manufacturers who have placed their devices at our disposal; the managers and workers in the industries who have coöperated in our investigations and offered opportunities to those whom we have trained; and especially, perhaps, the handicapped themselves, who have demonstrated their successful methods, offered their experience, voluntarily acted as subjects for investigations, and cheerfully followed all suggestions offered.

The progress in work for the handicapped along all lines is astounding. The coöperation between these various lines is highly gratifying. It is necessary now that the high standards set during the War be maintained; that the best practice obtained be standardized and universally adopted, and that the underlying principles which brought about the results be incorporated as an integral part of education both in the industries and out.

MOTION STUDY FOR THE HANDICAPPED

THE MAGIC OF MOTION STUDY

THE MYSTERY OF MANUAL SKILL ELUCIDATED BY A SCIENTIFIC STUDY OF THE BODILY MOVEMENTS AS RECORDED BY SPECIALLY DESIGNED MOTION-PICTURE APPARATUS—WHY "ALL CHAMPIONS BELONG TO THE SAME BREED"—A NEW METHOD OF TEACHING TRADES SO THAT EVERY WORKER CAN EASILY LEARN TO BE A SKILLED MECHANIC.[1]

WHEN Frank B. Gilbreth, as a boy, determined to learn the art of bricklaying in the shortest possible time so that he could have time to learn several other trades, he sought advice from the master mason at work beside him. At once he noticed an odd thing. Although the mason gladly showed him the proper way to handle and lay brick, he never followed this method himself. Again, the master mason had two additional methods for working, both different from the first: one when he desired to work fast and another when he was in no particular hurry.

---

[1] Copyrighted by Doubleday, Page & Co., New York, and reprinted with their permission, and that of the Editor of *Pearson's Magazine*. Written by Reginald T. Townsend.

This fact interested the young man greatly, and he watched the other men at work. The same held true in each case; each man had three, and often more, methods of doing the same work. This set the boy to planning as to the feasibility of adopting one, and only one, method of doing each kind of work, and thus to save unnecessary work and waste motion. Seven years later the boy—now grown to manhood and long out of the bricklaying class—had revolutionized the method of handling brick and was the recipient of a medal bestowed upon him by the Massachusetts Mechanical Association in recognition of his services in the advancement of scientific management in the field of bricklaying.

From that first step, thirty-one years ago, Mr. Gilbreth has devoted his life almost entirely to scientific management and the study of motions and the elimination of waste. Big, whole-souled, with a keen sense of humor and an unfailing faith in his fellow men, he has thrown his whole personality, an intense enthusiasm, and an unbounded vitality into his hobby—the study of motions and their application to industry.

And in the development of this study Mr. Gilbreth has cast aside old notions and apparatus, save where he could make use of them, and employed the most modern of devices to aid him.

STUDYING THE MOTIONS OF AN EXPERT TYPIST

The head and body of the typist are thrown up sharply against a black background divided into cross sections of known lengths, so that the motions made in operating a typewriter can be measured by the difference of position in each picture.

[face p. 2

Studying the

In its early stages his work was modeled more or less along the general lines of an efficiency expert.

Now, an efficiency expert is the "magician" of decreased expenses and increased production. He is the one who investigates the workings of a factory thoroughly, makes improvements here, omits stages of manufacture there, substitutes unskilled labor in place of more expensive skilled labor wherever possible, and, in short, endeavors to improve manufacture all around. Take the example of a girl folding handkerchiefs. Daily in the afternoon her work would slacken for some unknown reason and she would fall below her record of the number of handkerchiefs folded an hour. Here was work for the efficiency expert. Why should her production of folded handkerchiefs fall off any more than that of the many other girls at the same work? Investigations were made and it was found that the girl became fatigued sooner than her fellow workers. From what cause? More investigations, and it was found that she was sitting in an old chair the legs of which had become gradually worn down until she sat in such a position that it required an extra effort for her to hold her hands up at the proper level for folding handkerchiefs. Consequently she became fatigued sooner than her co-workers. So a carpenter was called in and he remedied the situation by nailing four blocks of wood under the legs of the chair, with the result that the girl's production is now kept up to capacity, with consequent gain to her employer, and if she chances to be paid by piece work, with consequent gain to herself and, moreover, no trace of unnecessary fatigue.

In his study as an efficiency expert Gilbreth came to the conclusion that the best way to learn a trade was to learn only the fundamental motions and to perform these rapidly, regardless of the fact that for the first fifty times or so the work done might be so far from perfect that the product might have to be cast aside as worthless. The elimination of unnecessary motions was far more important than spending time in learning a process thoroughly by a slow and elaborate method, for the time of a skilled laborer is far more valuable than the material wasted in getting his skill, and the increased production more than compensates for such a loss. Furthermore, the "slow and sure" method is actually a wholly different method from the method of the experienced, skilled workman,and in practical work is laboriously unlearned and the faster method learned by painful practice. Once an efficient standard of motions has been reached, so Gilbreth reasoned, fix that standard for all time by means of photographs and take notes on the time consumed in making

MULTIPLE FILMS

To reduce the cost of taking moving pictures of various operations in a factory, Mr. Gilbreth has patented a scheme whereby as many as sixteen pictures can be taken in the space of one ordinary picture on a film. By this method it is only necessary to develop one film and run it over sixteen times, observing one section at a time.

[*face p.* 5

these motions, recorded by means of a stop-watch.

For, when once a standard of motions has been made, it can be preserved for the use of future generations. Think of the number of processes—the so-called lost arts—of infinite value to humanity, that have been lost, merely because records were never kept of such processes. Gone is the secret of the Egyptian pyramid builders; forgotten are the ingredients of Greek fire; and lost, possibly forever, because it fell into temporary disuse, is the art of hardening copper, which to-day would be of immense value.

But the use of a stop-watch in the making of records of the time used in essential motions was not altogether satisfactory. The human element, always prone to err, enters too largely into the use of the stop-watch. Valuable time is lost in starting and stopping the watch and, besides, many machines work at a much faster rate than any stop-watch can possibly record. Gilbreth, working to overcome this difficulty, hit upon the cinematograph. What better way of observing and preserving motions could be desired than the moving-picture machine? With it no speed was too great to be recorded. (Mr Gilbreth's camera will take as many as forty-eight pictures a second.)

To record the time taken in performing an act a clock was invented that measured time down to the millionth of an hour, which, with a regular watch to check its accuracy, is included in every picture taken by the cinematograph, so that one is able to tell from the position of the hands in each picture the amount of time consumed in making a motion. Furthermore, the background and the floor in each picture is cross-sectioned into squares of a predetermined length, so that when a moving picture is being taken of any subject the body and head of the worker are thrown up sharply against these squares, and by examining the exact position of the worker in each succeeding picture in relation to these squares it is easy to determine just how much he or she has moved. The same holds true of the cross-sections on the floor to measure movements made by the feet. Temperature and humidity records, and signs giving the place and date on which the picture was made are included, the whole giving an accurate record of the exact functions desired.

These films, after they have been developed, are shown to the workmen, in order, to paraphrase the words of Robert Burns, that they may see themselves as others see them, and to criticise their own methods and learn the best way to perform their work. Viewing themselves or their co-workers actually performing

STUDYING THE MOTIONS OF THE "GIANTS"

In an endeavor to ascertain the likenesses in dissimilar functions and to discover the fundamental basis of their superiority, Mr. Gilbreth is studying the motions of various experts. For this purpose athletes, bricklayers, pianists, bookkeepers, surgeons, and fencers in action have been photographed in moving pictures. In photographing the above game of baseball many illuminating facts were recorded, and incidentally that the speed of the ball when flung by the pitcher to the batter varied from 210.07 ft. a second, or two and two-fifth miles a minute, up to a velocity of 2.8 miles a minute.

FOR TIMING MOTIONS

The device which can register a millionth of an hour. This clock and a regular watch to check its accuracy are included in each picture to record the time required to make each motion.

[*face p.* 6

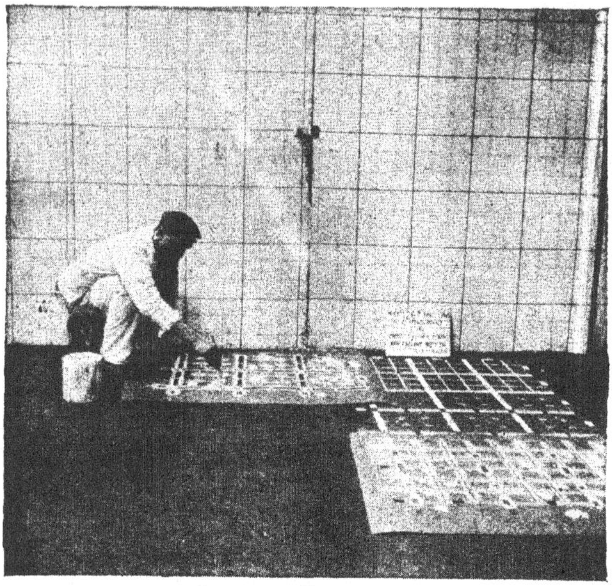

Charting a Background

The floor and the background of each picture are divided into cross-sections of a known length.

Mr. Gilbreth's Desk

Divided into cross-sections for studying the location of articles used by the occupant.

[face p. 7

operations gives them a new viewpoint from which to examine their work, which heretofore they have always taken as a matter of course. These films can be run as fast or as slowly as may be desired and the film may be stopped altogether at any point to examine the details of a picture more closely. It has been proved that many a workman, too timid to address remarks to an audience, is not only quite willing but eager to criticise in a darkened room the methods of the worker on the screen.

But the cost of using many thousand feet of film in recording the workings of a large industry was an element to be considered. Mr. Gilbreth solved the problem by devising a plan, on which he has obtained a patent, whereby the moving-picture camera takes as many as sixteen pictures in the same space on the film on which it formerly took one. So all that it is necessary to do is to develop one reel in place of sixteen and run the film over sixteen times, letting the audience study only one division at a time.

In connection with the cinematograph used with the cross-sectioned background Gilbreth devised what he calls the penetrating screen. It has been conceded that no two bodies can occupy the same space at the same time. Gilbreth proceeded to refute this theory! He set up a cross-sectioned screen and took moving pictures of it. Then he reversed his film and photographed the action to be measured, on exactly the same film ; and as the body of the worker, which stood out against the cross-sectioned screen, occupied a different position in each picture, knowing the length and breadth of the squares it was easy to ascertain the length of the worker's movements.

But the value to the manufacturer of the cinematograph in standardizing the proper way to perform work does not lie merely in taking moving pictures of workmen. It can and has been used successfully on machines. For instance, Gilbreth took a series of pictures of a braiding machine (a machine that weaves braids or shoestrings). In viewing this film he noticed that the method was not all that could be desired, and that the separate threads, which go to make up a braid, had a tendency to break off now and then, due to the fact that they were alternately held loosely by the machine and then tightened up quickly. Every such breaking of the thread caused a shutting down of the machine and loss of time, until a new thread could be substituted. Whereupon Gilbreth devised a method which, by means of an iron ring, kept all the threads at a uniform tension with an increase of at least 75 per cent. in the production of each machine—a tremendous increase in the output of the factory where many such machines were employed.

Mr. Frank B. Gilbreth (facing the camera)

Scientific student of motions, who, in studying the motions of workers with the cinematograph and stereoscope, has achieved great success in increasing human efficiency.

[*face p.* 8

In the Laboratory

Motion pictures of the entire workings of a factory were obtained, with the result that production was greatly increased.

Exhibiting a Film

To an audience of working-men so that they may study and criticize the methods of the worker. The film may be run as slowly as is desired or stopped altogether to illustrate a point.

[*face p.* 9

However great the steps taken forward in the study of motions by the cinematograph or micromotion process, it was still not altogether perfect. It permitted the making of accurate and satisfactory records of the methods used, but it did not visualize clearly enough the path taken by the motions, for the average individual has but a very small capacity for retaining in his mind's eye a complete picture of the various motions employed in performing an act. Consequently Gilbreth devised a method for defining the motions made in performing an act more clearly by attaching a small electric light to the worker's hand, or other moving part of the body to be studied, and taking a time exposure of the actions made. Thus the path of the motions in performing an act was clearly distinguishable by the line of light on the plate. By taking such a photograph with a stereoscopic camera one was enabled to view the path of the motion in three dimensions, length, breadth, and depth. But this line of light failed to show the time occupied in making motions, nor did it show in which direction motions were made. The time was indicated by putting an interrupter in the light circuit so that, instead of a steady line of light, there were a series of spots of light that flashed out at an even rate. Now, as it is known exactly how many spots of light are flashed a second and as the time between spots is also fixed, it is easy to determine the rate at which work is being done and the amount of time consumed in doing it. The registering of the direction of motions made was accomplished through the electric lighting current. By the quick lighting and slow extinguishing of the lamp the spots of light became blunt at the front and pointed in the rear, indicating the direction much as an arrow would. By the use of different time and speed dots it has been possible to attach lights to various parts of the body of a person performing an action and so to have on one plate a complete record of the parts of a person's body used in that action. Thus, in fencing, the demonstrator might have a lamp in each hand and one at the end of his foil, with another on his head, recording absolutely the motions made by head, hands, and foil.

To view such a photograph properly and to have an audience, such as a workmen's club, correctly observe the motions, the photographs should be examined through a stereoscope. The stereoscope, which enjoyed much greater popularity in preceding generations, when it was a novelty, than in the present one, is an optical arrangement of lenses, somewhat similar to an opera glass, which, if looked through, permits the observer to view the picture in three dimensions: that is, its length and breadth and, in addition, the salient parts of the photograph stand out from against the background exactly as they would if seen by the naked eye. This is called the depth of a picture. Now it would be somewhat difficult and expensive to supply each member of an audience with a stereoscope. So Gilbreth, by looking at the path of a motion through a stereoscope, and bending and twisting a piece of wire into the identical shape which the motion assumed, was able to reproduce exactly the path of light made on the photograph in a permanent form. In the case where speed as well as direction are to be shown, black and gray paint is used on such a model that has been painted white, the result being spots of white fading through gray to black, resembling closely the spots of light of the original. The wire model when completed is placed in a black box cross-sectioned in white, these cross-sections being placed in the same relative places as are the original cross-sections. So by means of these wire models it is possible to concentrate the minds of a group upon individual subdivisions of a motion which they in all probability could not do by examining a chart through individual stereoscopes. What the phonograph has done for music lovers, in reproducing and standardizing the best that there is in music and placing it at their disposal, these wire models have done for the skilled mechanic in aiding his study of efficiency. By studying these models, a set of which are on exhibition at the Smithsonian Institution in Washington and in the Psychology Laboratory of Brown University at Providence, R. I., the worker is able to see clearly what he lacks of perfection in performing the motion and to take the necessary steps to remedy the deficiency.

Now in many industries there are secret processes known only to the manufacturers themselves which they would not care to disclose, or in some cases the superintendent of a factory might wish to determine by himself the exact number of motions needed to perform certain work. In either case, by the use of an automatic attachment which is worked by merely pushing a button, one can take his own picture and make an accurate chart of his motions. Such a scheme is called, in the language of the science, an autostereochronocyclegraph, a term which sounds formidable but if divided into its fundamental parts is very simple: *auto*—automatic; *stereo*—stereoscopic, that is, giving the three dimensions; *chrono*—the Greek *xponos*, or the time element; *cycle*—the complete movement; and *graph*—the chart.

Then, in addition, should the manufacturer wish to make charts of the actual work of his employees without interfering with their accustomed routine,

EXAMINING A FILM

A stop watch is inaccurate and too slow to time many actions, but the cinematograph will take as many as 48 pictures a second.

TAKING MOVING PICTURES OF THE CHAMPION TYPIST

To learn what made her Champion. By such studies skill in one trade can be transferred to another, although it be of a totally different nature.

[face p. 12

Tracing a Motion.

By means of an electric light attached to the hand, or other working member of the body, the path of motions made in performing an act can be traced on a photograph.

Setting Type

Through a similar photograph it was found that the typesetter's left hand failed to cooperate with his right hand in filling a type-stick.

[face p. 13

or for the recording of surgical operations when a moving-picture operator would be seriously in the way, Gilbreth's device could be employed with a telephoto lens, in connection with an automatically operated cinematograph, which not only photographs objects at a great distance but photographs the time clock at a distance of only twenty feet at the same time.

The value of such autotele time study (as the method is called) is greatly lessened at times, owing to the absence of human coöperation on the part of persons who may be unconscious that they are being photographed. The coöperation of the workers, so that they may perform their work methodically and distinctly, is essential to obtain a clear negative which will illustrate strikingly the points to be emphasized for an audience. Mr. Gilbreth is, however, strenuously opposed to any secret time study and to the making of any motion observations in which the worker is not willingly coöperating.

When once the results of these studies, the micro-motion, the stereoscopic charts, and the wire models, have been determined, they are diagrammed on cross-sectioned paper called a simultaneous motion cycle chart. Such a chart records the time vertically and the working members of the body horizontally. These latter are subdivided into their constituent parts, such as, in the case of the leg, the thigh, knee, calf, ankle, heel, and toes. Now a complete cycle in making a motion consists of sixteen distinct elements as follows: (1) Search; (2) Find; (3) Select; (4) Grasp; (5) Position; (6) Assemble; (7) Use; (8) Dissemble, or take apart; (9) Inspect; (10) Transport, loaded; (11) Position for next operation; (12) Release load; (13) Transport, empty; (14) Wait (unavoidable delay); (15) Wait (avoidable delay); and (16) Rest.

When the motions have all been listed, the chart, when read downward, presents, in chronological sequence, the various activities performed by any member of the body, the posture taken during the action, and the time consumed; while, if read across, the chart gives a record of all the working members of the body at any one time and enables one to see which parts of the body are working most and which are being delayed. Such a system of simultaneous motion charts has been of the utmost value in permitting workmen to visualize graphically their efforts, with a consequent lessening of waste and with increased efficiency.

A striking example of the success which Gilbreth has achieved with the cinematograph and stereoscope has been with a large New England manufacturer. Here, taking pictures of men at work on a drill press, he noticed that the workers stopped to turn in

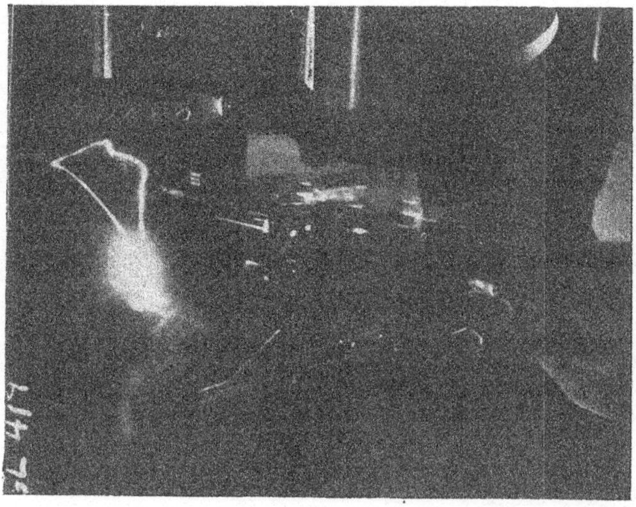

OPERATING A TYPEWRITER

The path of light clearly shows the movement made by the left hand in shifting the carriage of the typewriter back when the end of a line has been reached.

MOTIONS OF PLAYING A PIANO

A part of a series of studies to find out how far the motions made in such work as playing a piano, operating a typewriter, or an adding machine are similar.

[face p. 14

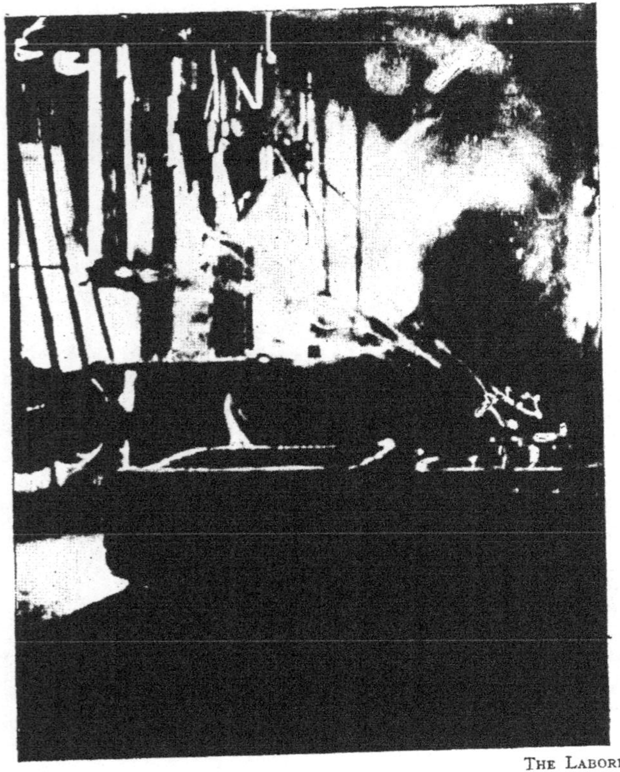

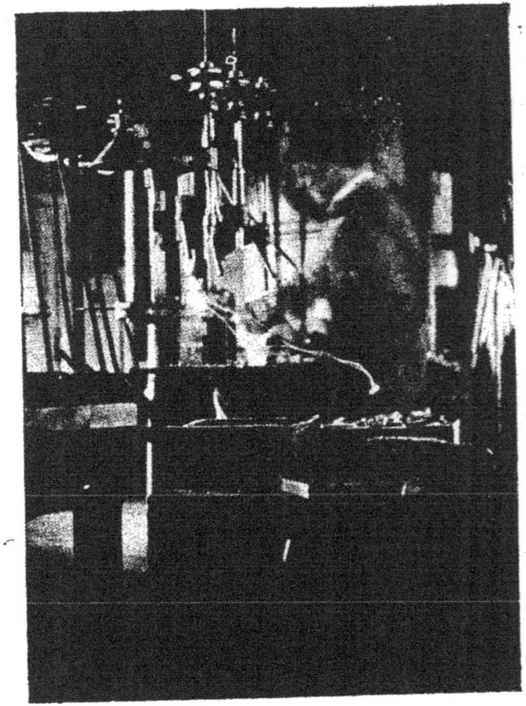

THE LABORER AT WORK

The picture on the left shows the laborer's motions when first using a drill press. The picture on the right shows motions after several attempts. The path of motion is more defined but indicates hesitation, and lacks the determination of a man who is accustomed to making decisions.

[face p. 15

mid-air the piece that they were to drill. While this resulted in a loss of time which by itself was of no consequence, when multiplied by the thousands of pieces to be drilled daily it amounted to a considerable loss. As a result of this discovery the pieces now all come to the man at the drill press arranged in proper position.

However, Gilbreth is not yet satisfied with the results of his discoveries. He is continually experimenting and devising new schemes, and even in his own home he applies his theories of measured functional movement. In this he finds an able collaborator in his wife who, last year, found time enough from bringing up six vigorous youngsters and managing the household to obtain a degree of Ph.D. from Brown University.

At present Gilbreth is busily engaged in studying the likenesses between human activities, as he believes that too much time has been wasted already in studying their differences. That is, Mr. Gilbreth believes that skill in all trades, in all forms of athletics, and even in such professions as surgery, is based on one common set of fundamental principles —the principles of economy of effort and rhythm of motion. In other words, all champions belong, in a sense, to the same breed—they unconsciously use exactly the same methods to achieve their exceptional results. It is not always wise to say this, however. For example, the prominent surgeon is perfectly willing to be photographed performing a delicate operation, but when the fact is mentioned that this is being done to find the similarity between his actions and those of other skilled workers, he becomes scornfully incredulous. How can such a thing be? He, a skilfully trained, highly developed product of many long years of study, to be likened to a machinist or a bricklayer? The thing is preposterous! But that makes no difference to Gilbreth; all skilled work, whether it be that of a surgeon or a stenographer, looks alike to him, and he keeps on filming experts and adding proofs that the same principles of motion underlie manual skill of all kinds.

Mr. Gilbreth has set out to take moving pictures of as many champions or experts in various trades or sports as he can, in order to study their methods and find the points of similarity between their motions. So the champion typist of the world, an expert bricklayer, and Christy Mathewson, the famous baseball pitcher, have been photographed; and a few months ago, in Germany, Gilbreth took pictures of the champion fencer of the world. He even hopes to get pictures of the champion oyster-opener of Rhode Island!

THE MASTER AT WORK

The upper picture is his first attempt' to operate a machine in many years. The lines of motion are clear but he hesitates, as the exact method has not come back to him yet. The lower picture shows a clear line of

FAMILIAR MOTION
The short, sharp line of motion made in removing a pencil from the upper left-hand waistcoat pocket, its accustomed position.

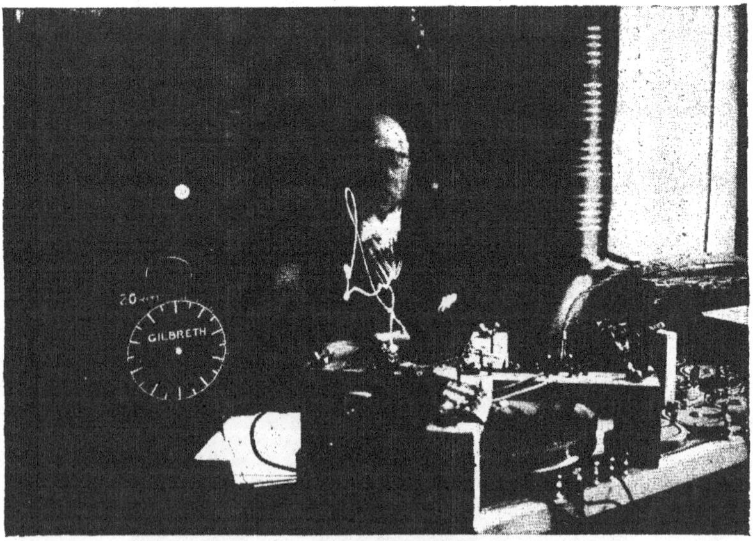

UNFAMILIAR MOTION
The hesitating, intricate line of motion made in removing a pencil from the upper right-hand waistcoat pocket, an unaccustomed position.

[face p. 17 (A)

Before

The motions made in loading sixteen boxes on to a truck before the method has been studied.

After

The motions made in loading the same sixteen boxes on to a truck after the method had been studied.

[face p. 16 (B

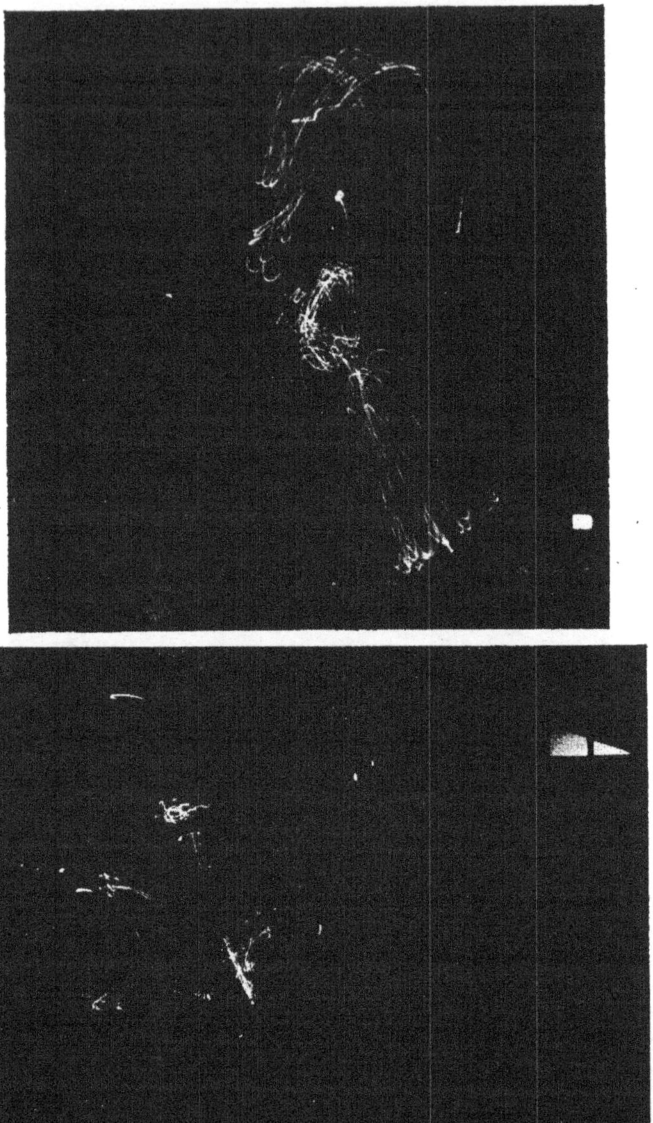

THE RESULT OF SKILL

The path of light made by the rapier of the champion fencer of the world. Note what little variation there is in the many complete cycles of motion, due to skill acquired by long practice in this sport.

[face p. 17 (B)

In the Hospital

Mr. Gilbreth taking a moving picture of a delicate operation to study the motions of the skilled surgeon at his work.

[face p. 16 (c)

THE AUSTOSTEREOCHRONO CYCLEGRAPH

A device which permits one to take moving pictures of one's own motions in performing an action.

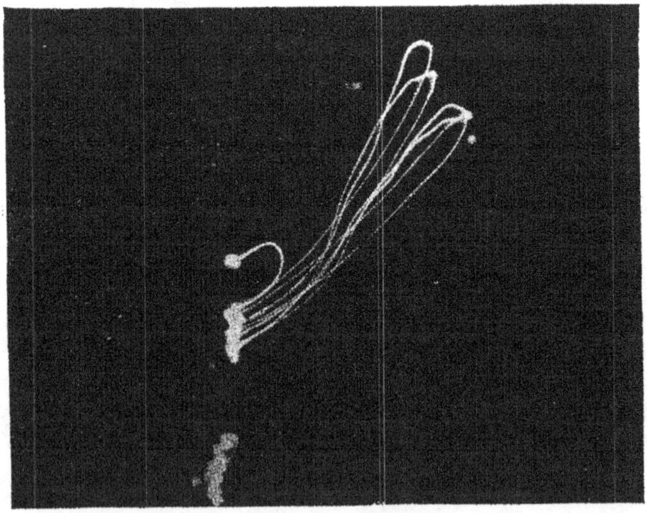

SEWING UP A WOUND

The path of the motions used by a surgeon in sewing up the wound after an operation for appendicitis. Note the clear, decisive lines of light.

[face p. 17 (c)

Although this study of the motions of experts has been under way only a short while, it has already yielded such important results in the finding of similar fundamental motions that Mr. Gilbreth is sure it will advance the cause of scientific management and measured functions as far again as it was before he entered the field of autostereochronocyclegraphology.

And the field for this advance is as wide as the applications of skilled labor itself. The waste of effort, the waste of time, and the reduced output due to unnecessary and unskilled motion are almost beyond belief when studied closely.

THE RE-EDUCATION OF THE CRIPPLED SOLDIER [1]

THERE is no question more important, more interesting and more timely to-day than the question of education. It seems ridiculous to say that we are only now beginning to realize the importance of education, yet such is undoubtedly the fact.

Lack of education lies at the root of many of our troubles to-day, and wrong methods of education will account for most of the others. The great problems of waste and its elimination, that range all the way from the saving of the least bit of food or fuel material to the elimination of the needless losses of war, are all based upon lack of, or wrong methods of, education.

It is time that the world faced this situation squarely, and realized that not only for present prosperity, but also for future safety and happiness, we must acknowledge the importance of education and discover and standardize the most efficient

---

[1] Presented at the Tenth Sagamore Sociological Conference, June 27-29, 1917.

methods, also that the time to begin the reconstructive work is Now.

It is with this broadest aspect of the situation from an economic, educational and waste-eliminating standpoint in mind that we desire to emphasize the importance of re-education for the Crippled Soldier. Here we have a small branch of educational activity overwhelmingly prominent just now, that gives us an opportunity to demonstrate what can be done with efficient education and the effects of such education upon eliminating waste.

The need for re-educating the crippled soldier is self-evident. We have, in many countries of the globe to-day, the economic balance destroyed or threatened by the sudden withdrawal of the fighting men of the country. These, if they return at all, come back, many of them, changed, to a greater or less extent, in capabilities and demands. We have men of all types of education, or without education, crippled and wounded, and placed suddenly and without preparation in situations where their previous training, in its specific aspects, seems to stand them in little stead. This is especially true of those who have only a manual education, since when they are physically disabled they find themselves unable to adapt themselves to new occupations without considerable assistance.

The world needs the work of every person existing and able to be a producer, but most important of all is the cripple's own need for constructive activity, and for feeling that he is still able to do " a man's job " in the world.

It is most necessary to emphasize that while the re-education of the crippled soldier affords a most excellent place for demonstration as to efficient educational methods, it is no field for experimenting. Fortunately such experimentation is not necessary. Efficient methods of education have been worked out, and all that is needed now is the energy and skill to apply them. Having studied the problem of the crippled soldier abroad, both thru actual observation and thru correspondence with the foremost scientists engaged in the re-education there, and knowing the needs, we have worked out in the laboratory the methods by which suitable occupations for cripples of any type may be determined and also methods by which training in these occupations may be transferred to the crippled learner.

This has been done thru Simultaneous Cycle Motion Charts and Motion Models, which embody data gathered thru the application of the micro-motion method, and the cyclegraph method of recording data.

With these methods it is not necessary that

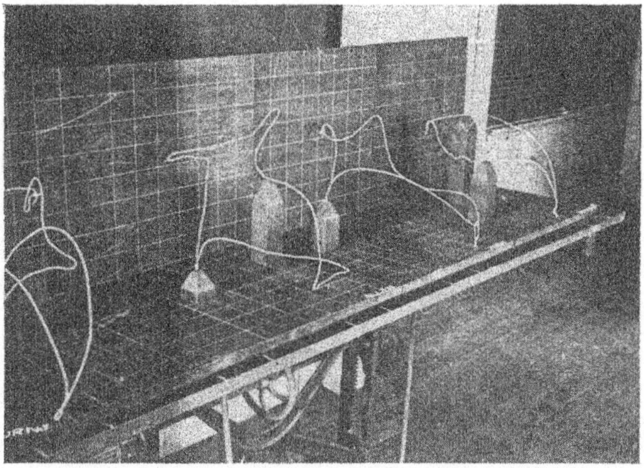

STANDARD WIRE MODELS

What the phonograph has been to the music lover in standardizing and aiding the study of music, these wire models have been to the mechanic in aiding the study of skilled motion.

THE TIME AND SPEED OF A MOTION

By means of black and gray paint the time, speed, and direction of a motion, can be shown on white painted wire models. In a photograph this result can be obtained by the use of intermittent flashes of light.

[*face p.* 20

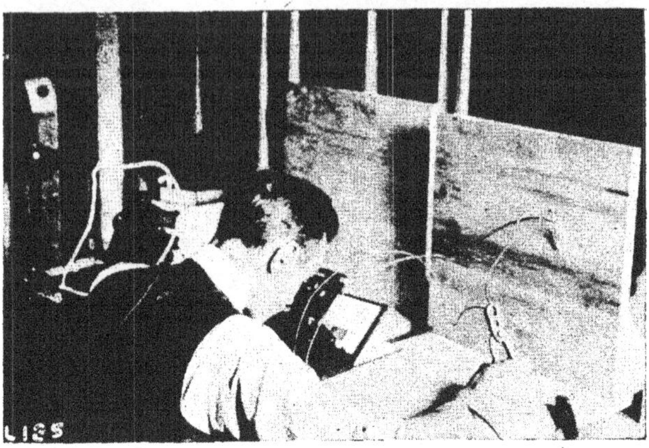

Making Wire Models of Motion

By examining a path of light in a photograph through a stereoscope the motion of an action can be reproduced in such tangible form as a wire model.

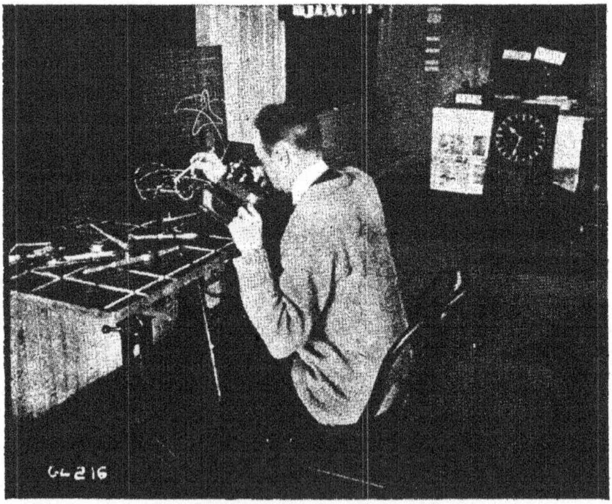

At Work on a Model

Painting the black and gray spots on a wire model to indicate the time and speed of a motion.

[face p. 21

experiments be made on the cripples themselves. The experiments, many of which have already been made, can be made upon unmaimed learners or workers, and, thru the devices, the data from these experiments can be incorporated into data to be used for the cripples.

We have been fortunate in having secured quite splendid coöperation in making these investigations —the Hon. John Barrett, Director of the Pan-American Union, having been one of the first to demonstrate to his own satisfaction and that of others the possibility of performing activity usually considered " two armed " with but one arm.

The advantage of experimenting with the unmaimed subjects is that they possess to an exaggerated degree the awkwardness that characterizes the recent cripple. Hence methods that succeed with them succeed with even greater ease and speed when applied to the maimed worker who has become accustomed to lacking various working members.

The methods, therefore, are ready. It is trained teachers that we lack.

There are various methods by which we may prepare these. One is by coöperating with those who are re-educating cripples abroad. This might be done by sending those who are to do the teaching here into the foreign field to see what is being done. This method has the disadvantage of necessitating sending people to some distance to acquire their information, and a further disadvantage, in that much of the work in foreign countries, because done without adequate preparation, is really not fit to be used as a model for our work here. Therefore it seems best that the training be done here in this country, under laboratory conditions. The industries furnish ample supply of cripples of all types who may be used as sample learners if such are desired, with the added benefit to these individuals and to the industries to which they will return.

We have been fortunate here also in obtaining coöperation from industrial workers who have eagerly embraced the opportunity to make their experience of use to others.

It is perhaps but natural that there should be a feeling in this country that, with so many pressing problems, the problem of the cripple can be left until such time as the cripples do return. Such an argument is, however, very misleading. The chief errors into which the countries abroad have fallen have arisen from the fact that this very thing was done, that the solution of the problem was postponed until the return of large numbers of cripples made some sort of solution necessary. The result was "hit-or-miss" attempts to better conditions that have left much to be desired.

These all demonstrate the necessity for beginning the work *now*. It must be begun from various standpoints; first, those who are to teach the cripples must be thoroly trained, both in the schools and in the industries. Second, a thoro survey of industrial opportunities must be made both by trained survey makers who have received special instructions as to what is needed, and by those in the industries themselves, who must furnish the largest amount of the data, if this is to be accumulated with the greatest amount of speed. Again, we must make arrangements to have those trained in teaching sent to the base hospitals, that preliminary work in re-education may be undertaken as soon as possible. The moment a man is able to take his mind from the pain of his wounds, and perhaps even before this, the possibilities of re-education must be presented to him. Again, provision must be made for seeing that this re-education is done under military regulations, that is to say, it must not only be *offered to* cripples but it must be *insisted upon*, exactly as it is in the highest type of work now being done, that in France. Again, every mind of the country must be focused upon discovering opportunities for the cripples. We must realize that these are of three kinds. They consist

1. Of so adapting cripples to jobs already existing, or so adapting such jobs to cripples, that cripples may become competitors with the whole worker.
2. Of finding occupations that do not exist, but which should exist for public prosperity, and assigning these to crippled workers.
3. Of reserving certain jobs for cripples, and putting them in these jobs on a non-competitive basis so far as uncrippled workers are concerned.

This is one part of the educational work that must be done for the general public. Another is arousing interest in the discovery, invention or adaptation of devices that will make it possible for the cripple not only to have a productive and paying occupation but also to " fit back " into all the ordinary activities of life. These may or may not be attached to the maimed limb of the cripple. They may be such simple devices as a tilting box and magnetized hammer to make possible nailing with but one arm. The more activities the cripple can master easily the more capable he will feel, and be.

If the most efficient methods are transferred with the least amount of waste—and if as many things are taught as can be adapted to, and useful to, the cripple—the resulting " re-education " will not only " make good " in itself, but will offer a model for all education to follow.

MOTION STUDY FOR CRIPPLED SOLDIERS [1]

MOTION study causes invention automatically. In such motion study invention lies a solution of the problem of enabling the crippled soldiers to earn high wages in the industries after peace has come. The lines along which the inventions are to be made are determined by accurate measurement. Hence, the resulting invention is a permanent improvement upon the best practice known.

The problem of the crippled soldier is no new one, tho it is seen in its most impressive and exaggerated form to-day. Furthermore, the problem of the mutilated soldier is really the same problem as that of the worker injured by an accident in the industries, so far as the engineer's particular field is concerned. While the soldier is still wounded or ill, his treatment lies in the province of the doctors, nurses, convalescents' homes, and other agencies for immediate relief. When the soldier is discharged

---

[1] A paper presented at a meeting of the American Association for the Advancement of Science, in Columbus, Ohio, December 27, 1915, to January 1, 1916.

from these as having been healed or repaired—to as great an extent as is possible—securing his usefulness, efficiency and happiness becomes a problem for the engineer, the motion study expert, and for the industries. There are some who think that it is the duty of their respective countries to support these crippled and maimed defenders for the remainder of their lives, and to require no work or activity on their part. Those who have been in close touch with actual conditions know that the last thing in the world the sufferer wants is such enforced or continuous idleness. The great horror of the majority of injured soldiers is that of becoming non-productive members of the community, as men who have done their work and are allowed to exist on sufferance. It is to be hoped that they will get pensions, but the enormous debts of their respective countries will make such procedure extremely difficult. In any case, it is the duty of the engineer, for he is best fitted to accomplish results, to provide as rapidly as possible the means and ways by which these men who wish again to become workers may accomplish their day's work satisfactorily to themselves and to their families and friends, without undue strain and fatigue, and with the greatest possible amount of personal satisfaction. The crippled soldier is like any other crippled worker who returns to his occupa-

DEVICES FOR THE CRIPPLED

The rocking nail box will cause the shafts of the nails to fall between the slats of the bottom of the box. The nails will then be "positioned" head up. The magnetized head of the hammer will then pick them up by their heads, and a one-armed man with this device can do as much nailing and tacking and on some kinds of nailing even more than can a two-handed man without the nailing box.

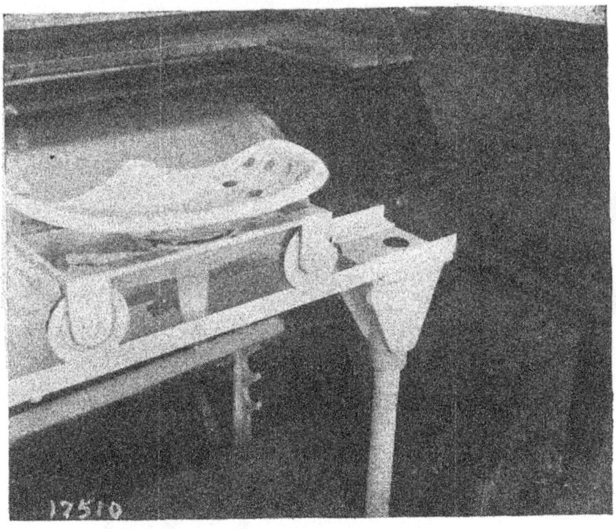

THE MARSHALL CHAIR

This device is particularly adapted to work of the cripple who is working at a machine or work place that requires travelling sideways. Like nearly all devices designed especially for the cripple it is also well adapted to the normal worker.

[face p. 26

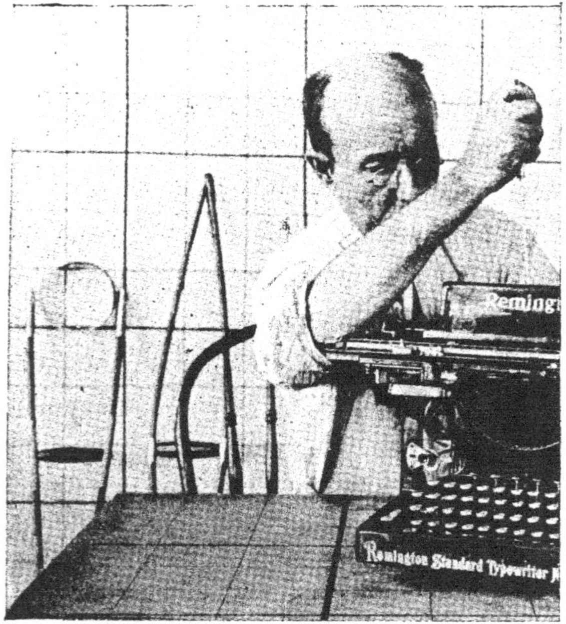

Special Devices for Helping the Handicapped

Mr. Case, whose picture is shown here, has had complete stiffening of many of the joints since 23 years of age. He is what is sometimes called a "hopeless case" because he has very little use of his legs and very little motion in his back and neck. He has, however, invented and made for his own use special devices such as peculiar shaped crutches, long handled hooks for pulling on his shoes, and tongs for pulling on his trousers, etc. He has learned two trades and is earning high pay as class model maker. His life is a fine example of what a cripple can do if what is left of him is of the right kind of stuff. *See also illustrations in frontispiece.*

[*face p. 27*

tion. He may have suffered, however, from a greater shock and have more horrible recollections. If so there is all the more need for providing him with proper and suitable work quickly, so that his mind may be taken from his own misfortunes and occupied with other interests; and all the more reason for making the work attractive, inspiring and stimulating.

The maimed soldier, if he has been an industrial worker, will, in many cases, the same as his mates in the industries who have been maimed during their work there, prefer to return to his previous line of work. With the remarkable mechanical artificial limbs that now exist this may be quite possible; if it is impossible, to as nearly that type of work as he can. This being the case, many workers can be best provided for by some change that will adapt the work to the man. This may consist principally of rearranging the surroundings, equipment and tools. It may consist of slight modifications of machinery. It may consist of changing the method by which the work is done, that is, of allowing some other work member of the worker's body to perform the motions that formerly were made by a member that is now maimed or missing. In any case the need is for invention. In similar situations the need has always been for invention, and the need has been met in the best manner available. Perhaps it was found that the work could be done sitting as well as standing, in which case the worker was given a chair specially designed to fit his individual requirements. Perhaps it was found, as in a case of typewriting, that a motion for moving the shift key, formerly done with the hand, could be transferred to the foot, or that the injured operator could use another make of typewriter having a double keyboard, thus requiring no shift key, and enabling a one-armed man to become a successful operator. Such a change as this meant both the redesign of the machine and training a new member to do the work. However, the limitations of such "hit-or-miss" casual inventions are evident. Unless an improvement in equipment were obvious, there was formerly no precise method for knowing exactly along which line the change in design should lie. In the second place, it was difficult to visualize which members of the body were engaged simultaneously in the activity, and thus transfer of activity from one member of the body to another was, consequently, also difficult. In the third place, there being no headquarters, no definite channel, for the exchange of information, the benefit of the invention was apt to cease with the particular individual for whom it was made.

The problem, then, becomes one of visualizing

Chronocyclegraph of Dr. Myrtelle Canavan working under the direction of Dr. E. E. Southard, Head of Psychopathic Hospital, Boston, Mass., determining methods of least waste in pathological laboratory practice.

[*face p.* 28

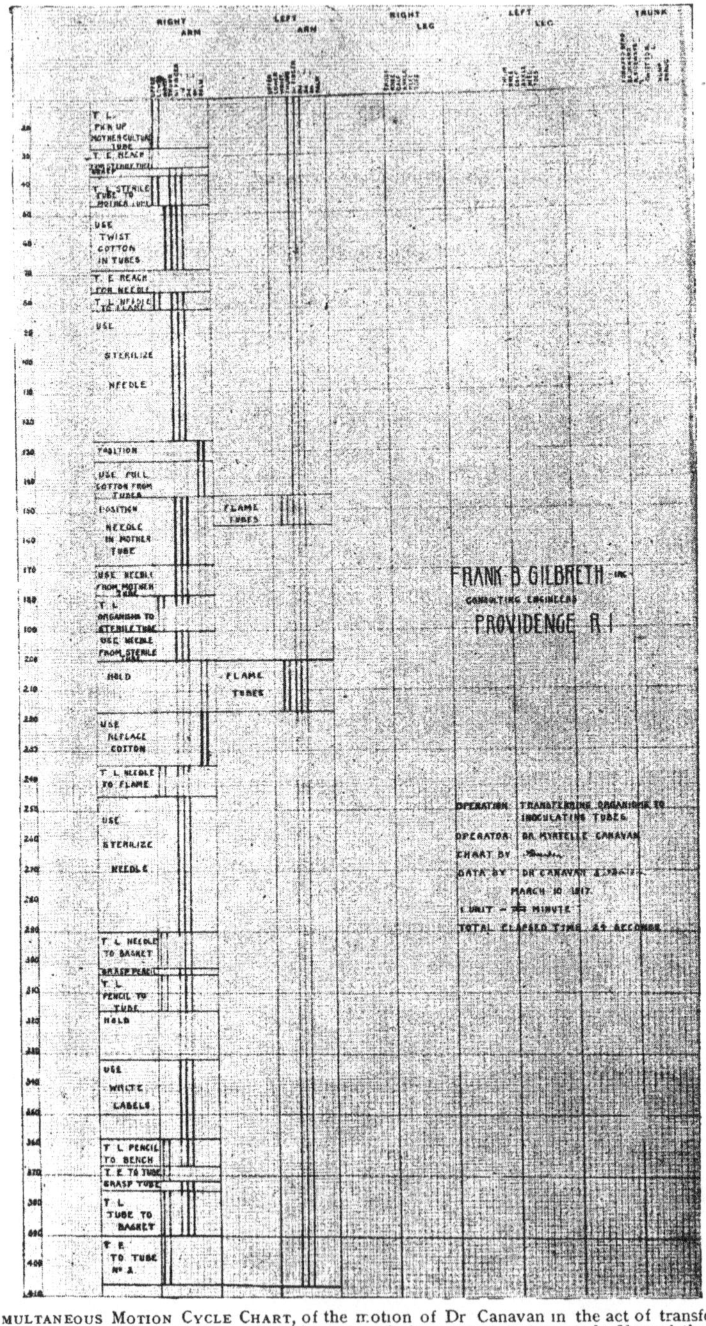

SIMULTANEOUS MOTION CYCLE CHART, of the motion of Dr Canavan in the act of transferring organisms to inoculating tubes. This chart is made from micro-motion study films of the same operation as shown here, also in the chronocyclegraph opposite.

[face p. 2

1. The existing surroundings, equipment and tools.
2. The best method for performing the work under existing conditions.
3. The standard or most appropriate type of worker to perform the work.

The visualization of the method (that is 2) enables us to see

a. The various members of the body engaged in performing the operation.

b. The motions and elements of motions used by these various members.

c. The relative and actual time consumed by each element of a motion.

We must be able not only to see these facts, but to see them all at the same time.

We have realized the importance of such visualization, and for years endeavored to obtain the device that would make it possible. This device we herewith now present in the form of the Simultaneous Cycle Motion Chart. This chart has been used by us in our work of installing Scientific Management and Motion Study in the industries and in surgery, and has been found applicable to all lines of activity where applied. In order to explain what this chart does, it is necessary to trace, tho only in outline, its history. Believing for years that the fundamental element in all activity is the motion, we started early to record the motions thru descriptions, thru ordinary and, later, stereoscopic photographs, and with the cinematograph. Thru this last, as we have before explained, in combination with the specially devised clock and the cross-sectioned background, we obtained satisfactory records of motions and elements of motions. We have in the micromotion films all the data necessary for complete visualization of worker, working conditions, and methods. There were but two things needed that were lacking in this record. One was a complete visualization of the entire path of the motion. The other was a visualization of the simultaneity of the different motions made by the different members of the body. It is difficult and practically impossible from the micromotion film, no matter how slowly it be run nor how often it be viewed, to note and hold clearly in mind what each member of the body is doing. We secured a satisfactory record of the path, direction and speed of the motion thru the chronocyclegraph records, and have, by transforming this chronocyclegraph into a motion model, made this path not only visible but tangible. These motion models are to be discussed before Section L of this Association, and, therefore, will be merely referred to here.

The Simultaneous Cycle Motion Chart overcame

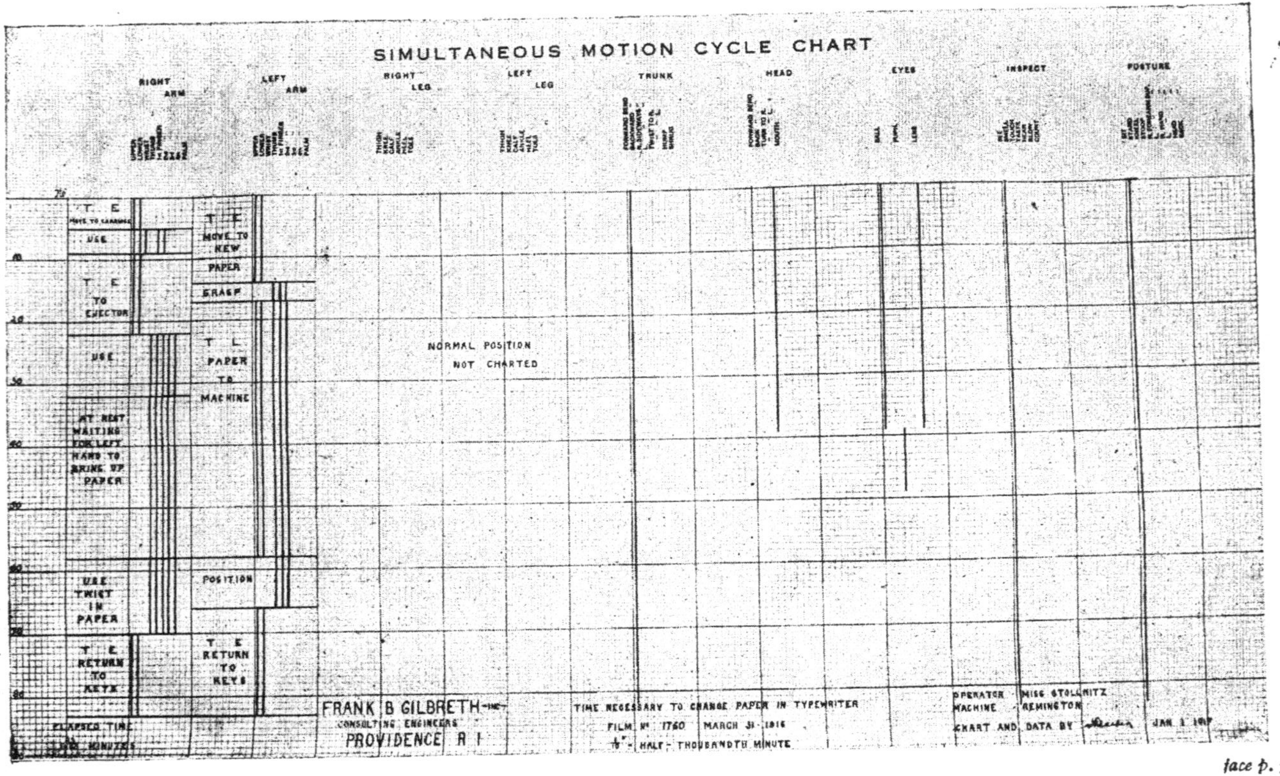
SIMULTANEOUS MOTION CYCLE CHART
RIGHT ARM
LEFT ARM
RIGHT LEG
LEFT LEG
TRUNK
HEAD
EYES
INSPECT
POSTURE
T E MOVE TO CARRIAGE
USE
T E TO EJECTOR
USE
AT REST WAITING FOR LEFT HAND TO BRING UP PAPER
USE TWIST IN PAPER
T E RETURN TO KEYS
T E MOVE TO NEW PAPER
GRASP
T L PAPER TO MACHINE
POSITION
T E RETURN TO KEYS
NORMAL POSITION NOT CHARTED
ELAPSED TIME
FRANK B GILBRETH INC
CONSULTING ENGINEERS
PROVIDENCE R I
TIME NECESSARY TO CHANGE PAPER IN TYPEWRITER
FILM No 1760 MARCH 31 1916
HALF-THOUSANDTH MINUTE
OPERATOR MISS STOLLNITZ
MACHINE REMINGTON
CHART AND DATA BY
JAN 1 1917

face p. 31

Simultaneous Motion Cycle Chart.

This Simultaneous Motion Cycle Chart of Miss Hortense Stollnitz, one time champion amateur typist of the world, shows the times of the sub-division of a cycle of motions for changing paper in her typewriter. The elapsed time is 71/2000 of a minute. She has since been enabled to reduce this cycle to 10 sub-divisions and the elapsed time to less than 2 seconds.

(For pictures from which this chart was made see *Applied Motion Study*, Fig. 5. (Routledge, London; The MàcMillan Company, New York.)

The methods of the champions should be taught to the handicapped even if they are not able to use the same method nor achieve the same times. The handicapped should not be taught merely "to do the work." They should be taught the underlying theory of the One Best Way.

The Cripple should be the medium through which all craftsmen may become acquainted with the One Best Way. The money so spent for teaching the handicapped would then serve a double purpose. Obviously the teachers of the teachers of the Handicapped are the ones who must first be taught. The remarkable increases in productivity resulting from such teaching will offset the expenditure many times.

[*face Chart*

the second difficulty. This chart is made by recording the times vertically, and the various working members of the body horizontally. The ordinary decimal cross-sectioned chart paper is used. The data for the chart is all contained on the micro-motion film. Because of the specially devised clock, recording intervals to the millionth of an hour and of any length desired, and the cross-sectioned background, we can read as small an element of the motion as the particular kind of work requires, and can immediately record it upon the chart. This chart is a motion cycle chart, because we have found the cycle the most satisfactory group of motion elements to handle.

A motion cycle consists of the following elements, arranged in varying sequence:

1. Search.
2. Find.
3. Select.
4. Grasp.
5. Position.
6. Assemble.
7. Use.
8. Dissemble, or take apart.
9. Inspect.
10. Transport, loaded.
11. Position for next operation.

12. Release load.
13. Transport, empty.
14. Wait (unavoidable delay)
15. Wait (avoidable delay).
16. Rest (for overcoming fatigue).

When the elements have all been listed, the chart, as is obvious, presents in chronological sequence, when read down any one column, the various activities performed by any member of the body, the posture during a complete cycle, and the time consumed by each element. When read across, the chart presents a record of all the working members of the body at any one time. Each of the seventeen elements of motion activity is represented by its individual color. This enables us to visualize certain desired groupings, and to see at a glance not only which members are working, and which are being delayed, are unoccupied, or resting; but at what they were working, and also to compare the records with records of similar motions in different kinds of work. The immediate use of these Simultaneous Cycle Motion Charts in the industries has been the discovery of the method of least waste, that is, the method of doing the work best fitted to become the standard method. This, of course, is always that method by which the most may be accomplished with no unnecessary fatigue and the least necessary fatigue to the worker. In other words, it enables us to find that method that will allow of the greatest saving of the worker and the greatest prosperity to both worker and employer.

Now, given a maimed worker, a simultaneous motion cycle chart is used

1. To adapt the method to the worker.
2. To assign the worker to an appropriate type of work, if he has no strong preference or aptitude for any particular kind of work.
3. To suggest inventions or changes that will make work and worker a better fit.

It is this "suggestion of automatic invention" that we desire to emphasize. Suppose, for example, that a worker who has lost his left arm desires to return to his former work, which is work apparently requiring both arms and both legs. We may find by looking at the chart that, say, two-thirds of his work is done by the right arm, the left arm doing comparatively little. We find that where both arms are occupied simultaneously, for a large proportion of the time either one or the other of the arms is engaged in "transporting empty" (Subdivision No. 14). Only for two short intervals are both arms occupied simultaneously. We see at once that it is extremely likely that the left arm's operations can be transferred, with a slight change in the conditions, either to the right arm or the feet, which, while listed as working, since they were standing, are really performing no activity resulting in product. This same chart, which, as illustrated here, shows the bringing back the turret head of a chucking lathe and positioning a new tool ready to cut, shows that the work could be done perfectly under the existing conditions by a man seated, thus not requiring legs for the work. On the other hand, should a man who had done this job lose both arms, it is at once apparent that he should immediately be transferred to some other type of work that can be successfully done without hands. An adequate knowledge of exactly how these charts suggest invention can only be gained by a close study of many of the charts themselves.

It must be apparent, however, immediately, that each element of the body and what it is doing appear before one on the chart something as the chess men stand on the chess board. One can study the board and plan the moves and note the possible opportunities. Those of you who are economists as well as engineers will immediately become impressed with the frightful waste in industrial conditions and will ask at once:

1. Why do we assign whole men to-day to occupations that crippled or maimed workers could handle satisfactorily?

2. Why do we allow a man to occupy so much time in performing work, when assignment of idle members to activity would economize the working time enormously?

3. Why do we allow the accumulation of unnecessary fatigue by work being done standing continuously that could be done sitting a part of the time, and by work being done with fatiguing motions that could be done as well with far less fatiguing motions?

The answer to all these questions is because it has not been common practice to think of these things, and because the economic and social pressure has not been so great, in the past, that the industries were obliged to think of these things. It is self-evident that with the astounding number, literally millions, of crippled and maimed soldiers who must come into the industries, we *must* think of these things and *must* act upon the results of our thinking. The ideal method of attacking the great problem of waste would be, of course, to start at the very foundation and reclassify all the trades themselves, according to the results of Motion Study. Each type of work should be analyzed into its motions and elements of motions. The motions should then be classified according to the amount of strength, skill and numerous other variables of motion study, that they require.[1] By this method of division of labor we are able to build up trades with definite manual and mental requirements. This enables us to assign each man to learn and to do that type of work which he could best perform with most profit to himself, to his employer and the community; but this is a change, of course, that cannot be made all at once. However, it is now being made more slowly than is necessary. All this only means more specialization. We can see plainly that the crippled soldier is going to bring this absolute demand for highly specialized work before the attention of the world. If a man has but one arm, if he has no legs, if he is blind, he must be assigned to some special type of work. The more work is specialized, the more quickly he can be so assigned, and the more thoroly he can get satisfactory results. There is still some fear, in many minds, as to the dangers of monotony due to specialization. This is not the place to argue that question. It need only be said that nothing is monotonous that is highly interesting, that monotony and fatigue are not synonymous, and that the remedy for so-called "monotony" lies not in supplying a different occupation, but in providing proper rest intervals, together with a sufficient

[1] See "Motion Study," D. Van Nostrand, New York City.

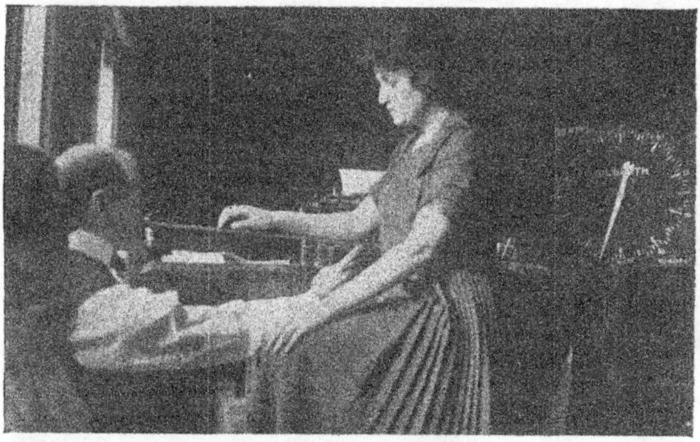

STUDIES IN THE ONE BEST WAY TO DO WORK

Mr. P. H. Waters in our Motion Study Laboratory teaching two typists who became champions in international contests.

[*face p.* 36

TYPICAL ENLARGEMENT FROM A MOVING PICTURE NEGATIVE

Pictures of a highly skilled secretary who has had many years of practice as a one-armed typist. Each of the pictures, or frames as they are called, of the moving picture negative can be enlarged for use as lantern slides. By this means the peculiar skill of successful highly skilled cripples can be shown for prolonged examination for teaching the One Best Way to beginners.

[face p. 37

interest and incentive. Remember, there is least monotony where the greatest skill is used. Reclassification of the trades, greater division of labor, and more specialization, these are coming and should come for the benefit of all.

The question now remains: What can we do now, to-day, towards hastening the day of their coming, and towards providing for the immediate need? The answer is: "Stimulate invention, and provide that this invention shall be from the best practice known at the present day." This means collecting:

1. All information as to how individual cripples have succeeded in becoming useful, efficient and happy.
2. All data on changes of machinery to make its use by maimed or crippled workers possible and profitable.
3. All data on the elimination of unnecessary fatigue, and the provision of rest for quickest recovery from necessary fatigue.

Start collecting such data immediately. Send it direct to any one you know who needs it. Send copies of it to us, that we may make it immediately available to the educators in all the warring countries, who are coöperating with us in this work of making their crippled soldiers happy, and also their enemies' crippled soldiers happy, in the least amount of time possible. We will immediately take this data, and, thru the help of the Simultaneous Motion Cycle charts, put it into such shape that it can be used not only to help particular cases like those from whom it was derived, but also to suggest adaptations and inventions that may help other different types of cases. The work of collecting this data may be ultimately that of an International Bureau of Standards. In the meantime, those of us who have actually seen the need firsthand, and heard the calls to help, must do what we can to see that available information is placed where it can do the most good. We can do more than this, in that we can arouse interest everywhere in the subject of Crippled Soldiers and Motion Study as a source of national wealth. No one who has not tried it can realize how extremely interesting all activity becomes when viewed and treated as a definite, measurable combination of motions and decisions. We have been astounded again and again to discover that someone who had lost a working member of his body is able, thru the loss, to find life more interesting, in that he has come to think for the first time in terms of motions, and how he can make his own motions more efficient. We are rejoiced to find again and again that some apparently hopeless cripple becomes actually more interested in life when he realizes the possibilities of motion economy and of utilization of motion possibilities.

We have here not only a mechanical problem, but also a psychological problem of cheering the maimed worker during his learning period, and of making the man feel the worthwhileness of what he can do. It is not necessary to go abroad to the battlefields or the hospitals in order to begin this work. Start with the first case you see, and make him feel not only the possibilities of what he can do, but the possibilities of what he has done. Let him feel that his experience makes it possible for him not only to add to the world's useful knowledge, but to send encouragement and assistance to someone similarly handicapped, that no unmaimed individual could possibly give. This has been done time and time again. This can be done in more cases than any of us realize. Take up, then, at once these two aspects of the subject of furnishing to the crippled soldier a means by which he can live and work, and you will have made, perhaps, the greatest contribution towards happiness minutes that may ever be your good fortune to achieve.

HOW TO PUT THE CRIPPLED SOLDIER ON THE PAY ROLL [1]

THERE are few problems before the world to-day more important than that of putting the Crippled Soldier back on the pay roll. If we broaden the term to include industrial cripples, we have a problem that affects all countries and all times. Because the war cripple appeals to popular sympathy, we are all vitally interested to-day in studying and solving this acute aspect of the problem, but our results are useable in the field of re-education of the injured of all types.

The problem of the crippled soldier is assuming greater proportions every day. The first stage of the solution of the problem is past; that is to say, in all countries has come a realization of the seriousness of the condition that exists, and of the necessity of doing something to better the condition immediately. With the knowledge of the seriousness of the condition has come a growing interest in the whole subject, and a desire to coöperate in putting these cripples on

---

[1] Presented to the Economic Psychology Association, New York, January 26-27, 1917.

a self-supporting, happy and efficient basis as rapidly as possible.

There are those who object to putting the cripple on the pay roll, feeling that he has done his part, and that it is the duty of society to support him the rest of his life. There are many answers to this objection. It is a question whether society can afford to support such an enormous number of non-producers, no matter how just their claim to support. Partial support may be possible—time alone can determine this.

The real answer to the objection is that the health and happiness of the cripple himself demand that he be kept busy from the earliest stage in his recovery period that he is really able to work, and that he be re-educated at the earliest possible moment. Reports of convalescents of all the warring countries show that the greatest problem is to persuade the man that life is worth living even in his maimed condition, and that he is still needed to do his part in the world's work. The injured man must be made to feel that he is not an object of charity, nor even a pensioner, but that he is a handicapped contestant in the world of active people, and that it is a sporting event what and how much he can do.

All who have taken part in or investigated work with cripples agree that it is essential that activity be attempted as soon as possible; the only question is, shall the activity be really productive or not. Surely in these times this is no question at all, and it is our duty to furnish real work to the cripple, work that he can do efficiently, and that will bring him returns in money, in satisfaction, in self-respect, and in the happiness that results from attaining these.

In order to do this we must:

1. Find types of work that a cripple can do.
2. Demonstrate to the cripple the advantages of working.
3. Find the type of work that the cripple can do and desires to do.
4. Adjust the cripple to the work.
5. Teach the cripple to do the work.
6. Persuade the uninjured man that it is hardly respectable to do work that can be done by a cripple.

These are all parts of the crippled soldier work, but it is not necessary to complete one part in order to start on another. In fact, all six of these are being done now.

We find work that cripples can do in two ways: first, by collecting records of cases where cripples have done various things; second, by studying the work of the injured workers, in order to find what members are used, and how the work may be reassigned to other members. This we do through the micromotion film and the Simultaneous Motion Cycle Chart, described on pp. 29 *seq.*, since they have been described already in available papers.[1]

We demonstrate to the cripple the possibilities and the advantages of working by showing him these records of both types. It should be noted here that the cripples are only too happy to be helped to be useful, if the re-education is begun soon enough, before they have to contend with the bad advice of the ignorant, though well-meaning, friends, and the difficulties of overcoming habits of idleness. This is really understating the facts. We receive constantly pitiful news of the desperate desire of the injured to be helped back to activity, and of the danger of the depression that inevitably results if hopes of re-education are not supplied immediately.

Finding the type of work that the particular cripple desires to do, and can be fitted to do, is largely a matter of tests that are at present being formulated and tried.

Adjusting the cripple to the work is done by two methods. These will be discussed in detail later.

The teaching is done through all the ordinary

---

[1] See "Motion Study for the Crippled Soldier," Transactions of the American Society of Mechanical Engineers, 1915 (the pioneer article on motion study re-education of the soldier); also p. 25 *sup.*

teaching devices, supplemented not only by micromotion films that show how the work is done and how long it takes to do it by elements and as a whole, but also by cyclegraphs, motion models, steroscopic photographs and charts.

The uninjured man need not be made the subject of a harangue on leaving such work as he can do to the cripple. The average worker teaches the world the meaning of true brotherliness, and will be more than ready to do his part in adjusting the industrial world to accommodate the new type of worker, when he realizes the need.

We shall now discuss the problem of adapting the cripple to the work in some detail, as it is one toward whose solution we can all contribute. There are two distinct methods of attacking the problem, both valuable, each being supplementary to the other.

The European method is well exemplified by the work of the famous French scientist, Dr. Jules Amar, who, in typical papers, considers the device or contrivance that the cripple is to use as the fixed element, and adapts and equips each cripple so that he can use the devices of his trade, or of the new work that he has chosen to do.

The typical American attitude is, perhaps, exemplified by our work in considering the cripple as

AN ARTIFICIAL HAND DESIGNED BY THE GREAT GENIUS, PROF. JULES AMAR, DIRECTEUR, CONSERVATOIRE DES ARTS ET METIERS, PARIS

We recommend to the attention of all workers for the handicapped the study of the wonderful works of Prof. Amar, especially *Le Moteur Humain* (*The Human Motor*), English Translation by Elsie Butterworth Daniels (Routledge); and *Organization Physiologique du Travail*, English Translation by Bernard Miall (The Library Press).

[*face p.* 44

PHANTOM PICTURE MADE BY DOUBLE EXPOSURE

Showing the total range of movement of the head and back of a one-armed typist, necessary to operate this combination, after a month's supply of paper providing for four copies has once been inserted for him. The shift key for making either capitals or small letters can be operated by either foot or knee or shoulder, or, if the typist has no limbs at all except one finger or one thumb, the shift key can be locked down with one motion, long enough to make the capital, and released again for the small letters. To attain still greater speed the shift key may remain in such locked position, thus making all letters capitals.

This machine is a combined typewriter and addition and subtraction machine. The same motion that presses the key to print the figure operates the addition and subtraction machine, therefore this combination offers to the legless, one-armed, one-eyed, deaf, stiff-backed cripple a chance to get back on the pay-roll, regardless of what he may also get as a pension. This machine is also especially adapted to the work of the blind on account of the simplifying of the handling of the carbon and manifold copies.

An accurate idea of the extreme range of motions can be obtained from the cross-sectioned background, the lines of which are four inches, or approximately ten centimeters, apart.

the fixed element, and adapting the device and method to the individual cripple who is to use it. It is but natural that the first method, that of the genius, Amar, should be used abroad, where many of the labor-saving devices in use come from America, or some other foreign country, and cannot be easily adapted. It is as natural that our methods should be in use here, where the devices are more easily changed, to suit individual workers, by the original maker of the machines.

As an example of the two methods, let us take the case of the cripple to be trained to be a typist. The Amar method is demonstrated plainly by the illustration herein included, furnished us through the courtesy of Professor Amar himself, whose coöperation on work for the Crippled Soldiers we are pleased to acknowledge. The other method we will describe in detail, hoping to arouse still further coöperation in this work in this country. Professor Amar's illustration shows a one-armed man operating the typewriter. We will illustrate the same subject and device as attacked by the other method by considering the cripple as the fixed element. In considering any type of activity to which it is proposed to introduce the cripple, we first analyze this activity from the motion study standpoint, in order to find exactly what motions are required to perform the activity, and in what way these motions may be adapted to the available, or remaining, capable members of the cripple's working anatomy, or eliminated by altering the device or machine itself.

Through a careful examination of the motions of many of the world's most expert typists, we found many interesting facts not generally known; for example, that the time required by the usual commercial typist to take out a finished sheet of paper and insert another in a position exactly level in the typewriter was about ten seconds. The time required to do this same work by Miss Hortense Stollnitz, the recent winner of the International Amateur Championship, is less than three seconds, while Miss Anna Gold, who won the National Amateur Championship, requires still less time. Our first thought, then, naturally, was to find and transfer the activity requisite for that shortest, most efficient, method to the work method of the cripple to operate the machine. We found that Mr. Casey, the one-armed secretary to the Mayor of Boston, could, with a simple device of his own invention, insert the paper with much skill, and that he operated the shift keys of his Oliver typewriter by means of foot pedals of his own design.

At this point we found, however, a device that

handled the paper in such a manner that all motions of inserting and taking out were eliminated from the ordinary work of the typist. With the coöperation of the leading makers of typewriters, such as the Remington, the Monarch, and the Smith-Premier typewriters, and particularly of Mr. George W. Dickerman, the devices were sent to our Motion Study Laboratory, where the motions of the machine and its operator were analyzed, measured and charted. How successful the results were is shown by the illustrations herein included. By means of this device, the one-armed soldier or industrial cripple can remove his paper and be ready with a new sheet inserted in place in two seconds.

When one original and several duplicates are made by the old method, the time required is, of course, longer for the commercial typist, because of the time and care required to handle the carbon paper and to keep the sheets of paper even and smooth. With the typewriting machine arranged for the cripple it takes no longer to handle two, three or four copies than it does to handle the single copy, because the duplicating is done by a permanent ribbon attached to the machine, and the trouble of handling the carbon paper is entirely done away with. If the rolls are kept free from the machine and hang on the wall, or other high support, they can be of any desired diameter, permitting a month's supply of paper if desired. The paper when attached to the machine is in rolls four inches in diameter. The process of tearing the paper into sheets of desired lengths is very simple, and can be done with one motion. The top and bottom edges of these torn sheets show an edge not quite as straight as if cut with the shears, but as straight as any paper torn against the sharp edge of a straight ruler.

Another example of the use of an existing device to facilitate the work of typing for a cripple is that of the double bank of keys such as exist in the Smith-Premier typewriter, and the use of a machine having all capitals and a single bank of keys as with the Remington or Monarch. By this means the motions of the shift keys are entirely dispensed with, and a legless, one-handed typist is enabled to equal the output of many of the commercial typists who are using but two of their ten fingers to-day; and a cripple with but a single finger can earn a living. We have also found dictating machines of use in decreasing the number of variables against which the typist works. When provided with a dictating machine, a typewriter requiring no shift key action and with the rolls of paper properly attached, a willing one-handed worker can compete successfully with the average stenographer-typist

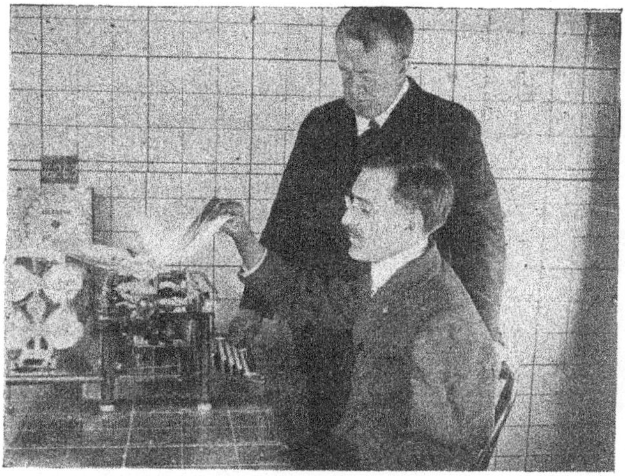

SINGLE BOARD TYPEWRITING MACHINE FOR ANY NUMBER OF SHEETS UP TO FOUR

No carbon paper is required, as ribbons serve the purpose, thus reducing the number of motions to a minimum. The magazine holding a week's supply of paper is attached to, and travels with, the carriage. The sheets may be torn off separately, or all at once, against the sharp attached straight edge.

This single keyboard machine can be used with capitals and small letters even by a one-fingered typist by locking the shift key down when a capital letter is required; but much greater speed can be attained if capitals only are used, tho this retards slightly the speed of reading of most people.

Single Keyboard Machine with Lockable Shift Key and Automatic Line Indenting Keys

For beginning the first word of a line at any point of the line with one motion of one finger. Any number of rolls of paper, up to four, are fastened to the wall or other support about two feet above the typewriter, thus adding no weight, and causing no slowing down of the movement of the carriage.

Double Keyboard Machine with Upper and Lower-Case Letters Requiring no Shift Key

The apparatus as shown here is for not more than two copies. No carbon paper is required, as a double typewriter ribbon serves the purpose instead. The top and bottom edge of the sheets that are torn off are straight and true enough for most purposes. They can, of course, be trimmed with shears or cutters if desired, but when it is understood that the torn edge is the handmark of crippled employment it will be rather desirable than otherwise. The rolls of paper can be printed with a letter head at the top and guide marks for trimming sheets to exact size if desired. If greater economy of paper is desired, the printing can be put in repetitive form in the left hand margin and the paper can then be torn off just below the last line, regardless of the length of the sheet.

with the old equipment, and perhaps in some cases be able to earn more money than before being crippled. He can, in a small office, handle successfully dictating machine, typewriter adding machine and telephone.

This use of, or adaptation of, existing devices by no means does away with the necessity of the most careful motion study and fatigue study of the operation. It is only thru these that one is enabled to classify completely the motions involved, and to discover which ones of these can be handed over to available, securable or inventable devices.

We have so far found all manufacturers of devices approached more than willing to adapt their work to the requirements of those who are maimed and crippled. We hope by offering this paper to arouse still further coöperation in the makers and users of devices, that they may think in terms of cripples during the inventing, manufacturing and using periods.

This branch of the work, like all the other branches, demands the most careful investigation of the mental as well as of the physical side. There are certain types that will respond quickest to attempts to use the regulation equipment, and will be willing to adapt themselves, even to their own discomfort, in order to use it. There are others who feel that it is their right to have all mechanical aids at their service. There are some who find artificial limbs, and especially mechanical limbs, helpful and interesting. There are others who have no use for any such devices, and who prefer to show their adroitness by doing, with their limited equipment, all or nearly all that the ordinary uninjured man can do. Each individual must be studied, and the proper method of treatment applied.

But it is the work of all of us to supply the data with which the experts will work. The individual histories of cases where cripples have been enabled to cope successfully with their handicaps must be collected. The data must then be compiled, properly classified and cross-indexed, and incorporated into a series of books, copies of which should be put into every large library in the world. This work would eventually pay for its cost of compiling and distributing, and no one can estimate the good that would be done by having every cripple feel that he had actually books of cases of men injured like himself to refer to for help and encouragement. The histories should be not only of those who have been recently crippled, but also of old cases of the handicapped who became skilled. They should also include those born handicapped, as well as those injured later.

The great need is that everyone shall realize that there is a part in the work for him. It is the work of the psychologist, of the economist, of the industrial expert. True! It is just as much the work of every man, woman and child in the community. It is active, practical, interested coöperation that is needed—and it is needed NOW!

THE CONSERVATION OF THE WORLD'S TEETH. A NEW OCCUPATION FOR CRIPPLED SOLDIERS [1]

THIS paper embodies a new aspect of the crippled-soldier problem, that of finding work that needs to be done and has not been done, or has been done inadequately, and assigning it to cripples.

In this age of destruction there is great need of conservation, and no conservation is so necessary as that of human beings. With the constant destruction of men in the great war has come the pressing need of conserving and using the cripples, both war cripples and industrial cripples. This is necessary for the good of the maimed themselves, as well as for the good of the world.

We may place the cripple by so changing his old work, by means of Motion Study, as to enable him to return to it. In many cases this is the best method to use, as it helps the man to "fit back" into

---

[1] Presented at the Consolation House Conference, March, 1917.

normal life, and demands little re-education.[1] Or we may place the cripple by so changing a type of work that he has never done as to make it easy and possible for him to earn a living. An example of this is the work made possible by so adapting the typewriter and other office devices as to allow a man of intelligence who has never operated them to earn a living and compete successfully with uninjured workers.[2] This is an excellent method where the cripple desires a new occupation and a new interest, or where the old occupation, because of its lack of adaptability, or because of the nature of the maiming, has become unsuitable or impossible.

Or, again, we may place a cripple at some new work, such as Dental Nursing, that has never been done to the degree needed—that is practically a new and a much-needed occupation, and thus not only employ him, but also conserve the energy of those he tends as well.

Dental Nursing may be defined as that part of prophylactic treatment of the teeth that can be done by a person without a complete dental training, namely, the polishing of the teeth by hand with a stick and pumice.

---

[1] "Motion Study for Crippled Soldiers," American Society of Mechanical Engineers, 1916. See *ante*.

[2] "How to Put the Crippled Soldier on the Pay Roll." See *ante*.

There is a world-wide lack of knowledge as to the relation of sound teeth to good health. America is recognized as the leader in the profession of dentistry. American dentists are recognized throughout the world as being, as a class, the most expert practitioners in all branches of dentistry; the other countries are now also coming to the front in this great human work. In spite of the great work of the dentist, even in America, and still more abroad, the care of the teeth is generally looked upon too often by the public as simply concerning appearance, beauty and comfort or speed in the process of mastication rather than as the most important factor of good health, while the dentist is too often interested primarily in filling cavities rather than preserving the tooth as a whole. The greater productive efficiency resulting from the natural use of all of one's teeth remains almost unappreciated. It is natural, this being the general viewpoint, that care of the teeth, or dental treatment, is often classed as a luxury rather than a necessity. The high cost of dentistry practically makes such treatment a luxury at present.

We find, then, that the average person:

1. Does not appreciate the importance of the by-products resulting from sound, clean teeth.

2. Does not realize that it is physically possible for nearly all to have sound clean teeth.
3. Does not know that the only reason that he has not good natural teeth is because of the present financial problem of high cost of "upkeep."

To be sure, there are dental clinics in all dental schools where one can get dental work done by dental students at a nominal fee, sometimes for merely the cost of the materials and in some cases for no charge whatever. But this is often extremely unsatisfactory, especially if the patients are workers who must lose their working time to attend clinics and secure treatment.

The work of the dentist is expensive, and must necessarily be. The high cost of dentistry is not surprising, nor is the profession of dentistry to be blamed for it. The training for the profession is long, arduous and expensive—and much of the work involves costly materials, as well as time, and provides problems requiring no end of education, experience and the highest grade of skill. Dentistry provides an unlimited, satisfying field for the mechanical genius. How are we to provide proper pay for such work, yet insure necessary treatment to the average wage earner?

The answer to this is:

1. By functionalizing the work of the dentist.
2. By having the trained expert do the skilled work only.
3. By training low-priced workers to do such parts of the work as require less skill.

The results of the functionalization will be:

1. Reduction of the cost of the cleaning of the teeth.
2. Clean, which means sound, or "near sound" teeth, within the reach of all.
3. Less need of costly work by the man unable to afford it.
4. Savings that can be devoted to such work, if it be needed.
5. Better health and added efficiency.
6. New work for the Dental Nurse, the cleaners of teeth.

There are several questions involved that must be answered. The first is: "Do clean teeth last longer than those not clean?" It has been proved time and time again that teeth can be preserved by preventive treatment. This is recognized to-day by all of the best dentists. Nearly all teeth are lost in two ways:

A. The teeth decay.

B. The teeth become loose.

Both decay and loosening can be almost entirely

eliminated by frequent cleaning with a toothbrush, with dental floss, and treatment by a thoro process such as by the stick and pumice of the operator. It is difficult to get most children and many adults to use a toothbrush habitually, but it is always easier to induce one with good teeth to use a brush regularly than one with poor teeth. Besides the daily cleaning it is desirable also to have frequent cleaning by a dentist, but the dentist cannot afford to give his time to do this cleaning at a price the worker can afford to pay. The result is that the great majority of people have their teeth cleaned by a dentist at periods rather more than less than a year apart.

Careful records of teeth that have been cleaned by a dentist once a month regularly for a long period of years, show beyond the slightest doubt that the number of cavities that occur are very few, and that these can be filled, while of small size, with little injury to the teeth and with little or no pain or discomfort to the patient. The bacteria that cause decay adhere to the surface of the tooth, then cover themselves with a film that is jellylike at first, and, if not soon removed, becomes a hard covering, under which the bacteria proceed safely to attack the tooth. "Decay" follows. Scrape the bacteria off before they attack the tooth and there is no decay.

The second question is: "Can the work of the dentist be functionalized as suggested?" All work can be functionalized, and most kinds of work are being. The work of the dentist is already functionalized much more than it was a few years ago, and is being divided more and more every year. For example, the dentist makes few of his tools nowadays, and dental laboratories are doing more and more of the mechanical work of the dentist. The laboratory specialists can do the work better than the "all-around" dentist, and can do it for him at a price at which he cannot afford to compete. In other words, the dentist, under the financial incentive, sublets certain work that relieves him of certain low-priced motions. Such are involved in the preventive operation of cleaning the teeth.

The third question is: "Can the dentist afford to give up this branch of his work?" There will be some objection from some quarters to this suggestion. Some will say that "the dentist needs the money." This is offset by the argument "the patient needs the teeth." "Our natural teeth belong to us, and we must decide."

Seriously, this new work will bring more, rather than less, work to the dentist. The barbers were aroused when they saw the rapid increase in the popularity of the safety razor. Yet the barber was never so prosperous as he is to-day. Shaving was a luxury in the days of Benjamin Franklin. It is now almost a daily necessity for most men. The care of the teeth at a price that all workers can pay will eventually make more work of that type for which their training fits them for the dentist. Those dentists whom we have consulted agree to this.

The fourth question is: "Will assigning this preventive work to others than dentists spread disease?" To teach Dental Nurses the principles of antisepsis is a comparatively easy matter. Moreover, they should be allowed to practise only after passing a proper examination, proving their ability, and then receiving a proper license. A complete "follow-up" system, such as is outlined by Dr. E. A. Codman of Boston for hospitals, should be installed, whereby each treatment should be recorded, and the records sent to the State Department in control of the work. This follow-up system, called the "End Result Record System," provides for making records of the patient and the treatment at the time of an operation, and requesting each patient by letter to report his condition one year after. Patients will not have the same objection to the recording of all particulars of dental treatments that they have in the case of medical treatments. Such a follow-up system "over-inspected" by the State Board of

Control would very materially increase the quality of the general practice of dentistry.

This paper is not on the subject of dentistry, except in so far as it discusses this separation of the function of cleaning for the prevention of decay. Nevertheless, the general principle, that inspection always causes an increase in quality, should be emphasized.

The fifth question is: "Would it not be extremely difficult if not impossible to teach the Dental Nurses the best method of doing their work?" In our work of installing management in the industries, we have found that problems that have always been considered very difficult become comparatively easy of accomplishment when the methods of the best workers have been recorded by the micromotion and chronocyclegraph methods, then analyzed, minutely measured, synthesized and standardized. We have found that the method of least waste never lies in the consecutive acts of any one worker. We have invariably found that a better method can always be devised than has been found already in existence. This can be realized in the case of the dentists, particularly because of the fact that being "lone workers" they have comparatively little chance to watch and to learn from each other, as do the workers in an office, shop or engineering undertaking, or other groups. Recording the methods of "lone workers" always brings out the fact prominently, that no two operators use the same method. Obviously their methods cannot all be the best. Our studies of the dentists who have coöperated with us bring out this general fact with surprising force.

Now, teaching the one best method known and presenting the method by means of standard instruction cards, stereoscopic photographs, chronocyclegraph, simultaneous motion-cycle charts, wire models and other devices and methods for the transference of the best experience and skill from those who have it, to those who have not, gives the learner at once, at the very beginning of his career, the knowledge of the best method known. This best method is based upon the actual measurement of motion study, and not upon the personal opinion or judgment of unmeasured experience. This does not mean that the worker so taught cannot deviate as his judgment later may dictate. He may deviate later for greater efficiency, and, on the other hand, he may deviate downwards, but at least he will first be taught and will learn that best method known, and will *always feel the call* and the constant interference of his habits first learned, and these are the best that can be found. This method of deriving and teaching the "best way" should be used by the

Dental Nurse, and we are prepared to furnish at cost to Teachers of Cripples, standard micromotion studies of a one-armed, one-eyed, legless dentist, cleaning teeth with most satisfactory results.

The sixth question is: "Would not the equipment for doing the work be so expensive as to prohibit many undertaking the work?" There is much work in the prevention of decay that can be done with almost no expense for equipment. This is vital to many patients; for, in the last analysis, they pay for the equipment, whether good or bad, whether expensive or inexpensive. If quite expensive, it is not apt to be easily portable, and they must pay also with their time in going and returning to and from the place where the non-portable apparatus and equipment is located. If portable, they may have to spend more time in the cleaning process. This, however, may be of still less importance if done outside of their working hours. A stick of wood—orange wood is particularly satisfactory, but many other kinds of wood are suitable—and a little powdered pumice will do remarkable preventive work in the hand of a properly taught Dental Nurse.[1] If a stick be used, the same stick should never be used on two patients. The stick

[1] We are indebted to Mr. George W. Dickerman for particularly efficient devices for this purpose.

should be thrown away, after it has been once used. The pumice, once poured into the dish, should never be used again; that is, only enough powdered pumice should be poured from the bottle to serve for one treatment of one patient. The Dental Nurse should always wash his hands thoroughly with good soap and hot water, *in the presence of the patient, both before and after a cleaning treatment,* particular attention being given to the crevices around and under the nails. An expensive dental chair is, of course, more comfortable but it is not at all necessary. It is better to perform the process on a log in the forest, on a mason's scaffold, on the front door-step, or in a barber's chair than not to do it at all.

This leads to the seventh question: "How can the people be induced to avail themselves of this service?" First, by making it fashionable, and by making it economically and hygienically indecent not to have teeth cleaned. Preventable loss of teeth must be made the badge of ignorance, personal neglect and indifference to national efficiency. Second, by holding parents criminally responsible for the condition of their children's teeth until the children are old enough to be responsible for caring for their own. Cavities found in children's teeth should be reported, and a follow-up system carried out, making neglect to have a cavity filled sufficient cause for a visit from a dental inspector similar to a truant officer, who would inspect and enforce the proper cleaning and thorough filling of all teeth. This may seem radical, but the far-reaching ill-effects of inefficient teeth are important enough to warrant it.

If statistics could be made of the loss of productive efficiency, to say nothing of the agony and loss of working time due to defective teeth, they would show the necessity of radical treatment of this important subject. The reason that but little has been done about the nation's teeth is because the possibilities of the subject are comparatively little realized, and the most necessary innovations have always come surprisingly slowly. The majority of people as yet do not realize the actual money value of their teeth. It is safe to say that every dollar saved on teeth at present is given several times over to a physician later, and the general cause of much ill health is traceable to the bad condition or absence of the teeth. Furthermore, few people know that most of the decay is easily preventable by proper periodical cleaning, and the rest of it can be taken care of by the filling of the cavities when they are first formed. A very large proportion of the people get their first knowledge of a cavity only when it is large enough to ache.

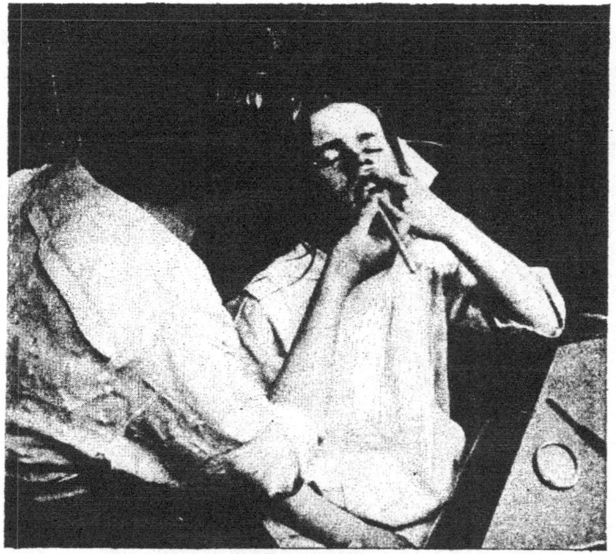

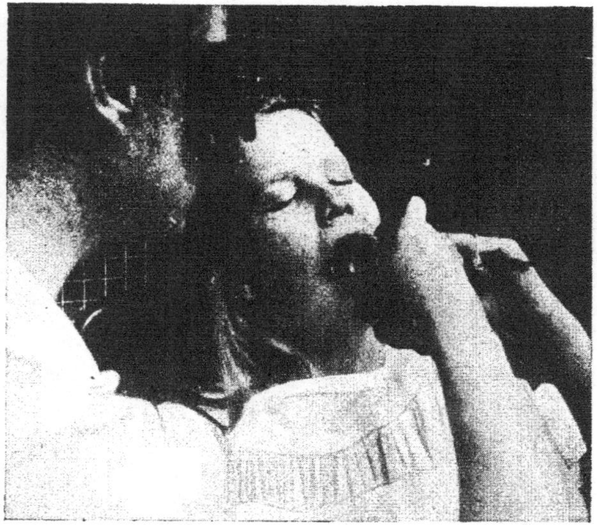

Dr. Jane G. Bunker, an expert dentist, demonstrating that the work of the oral hygienist of cleaning teeth can be done by a one-armed, one-eyed, and totally deaf operator. It has been found that the patient's hands can be used for holding the lips in the desired position and that the dentist's mirror can also be held in the desired position by the patient. There is every reason why the patient should "utilize his period of unavoidable delay" assisting in the work.

[*face p.* 64

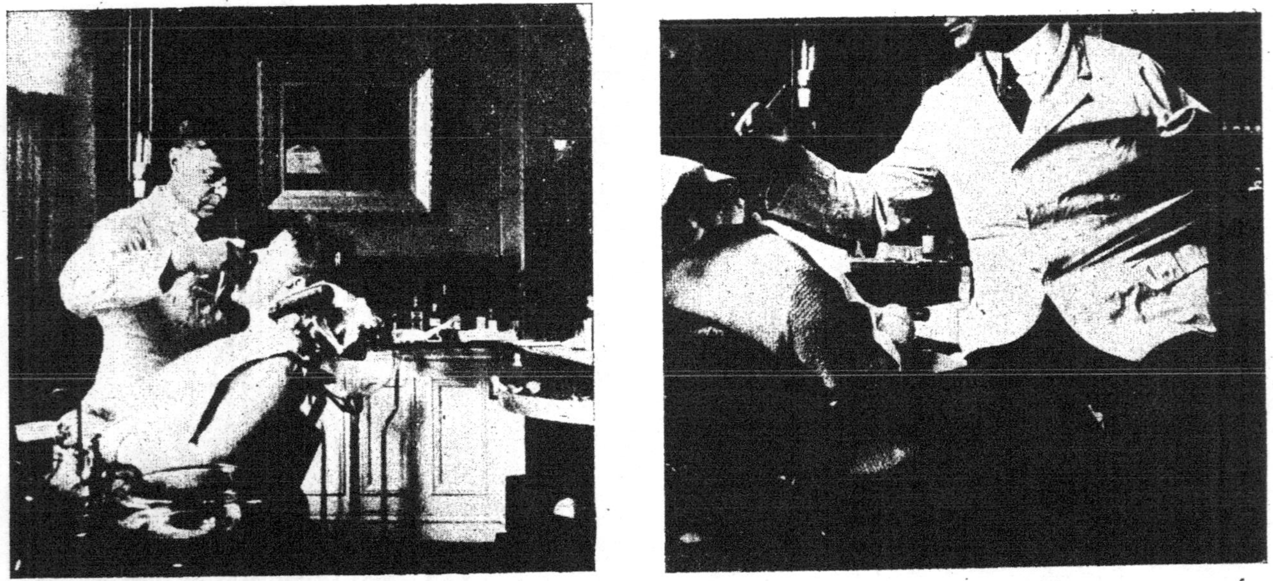

Dr. Frank L. Marshall, an expert dentist, demonstrating that a legless, one-armed, one-eyed, totally deaf operator can perform the work of an oral hygienist.

[face p. 65

The eighth question is: "Exactly how can this new work benefit the Crippled Soldier?" In our Motion Study investigations of the most skilled dentists who are coöperating with us, we find that the work of prevention of the loss of teeth can be done by an operator who has but one hand and no legs. Of course, it will be generally admitted that an operator will never be expected to do much of the operation with his feet. Nevertheless, most dentists stand when they are doing such work. It can be done quite as well sitting, and legs are not in the least necessary for the work. While a dentist uses both hands for his work, the patient's hands usually remain idle. Now, we find the patient can pull his own lips to one side perfectly well, and even hold the little mirror if necessary, though this is seldom, if ever, actually essential except for greater speed and subsequent inspection. We make this statement after having had dentists actually do the work to their satisfaction with one hand held behind their backs during the entire operation.

Thus this new and necessary work may be used to provide a livelihood for the maimed heroes of all countries who are being discarded by the great war. The livelihood will be better than most of them made before they were cripples, and the vocation will provide a most pleasant outlook that will assist in hastening the rapid recovery of many a man who sees that his disability will prevent his following his previous life-work. We believe that a totally deaf, one-eyed, one-handed, legless cripple properly taught can do more efficient work in cleaning than the dentist can do in the time for which the average worker can afford to pay. This is no dream for the future. It is a working plan which is being carried out to-day. The most progressive and skilled dentists whom we can find have consented to coöperate with us, all without pay, and will furnish the standardized instructions, derived by means of the methods of measurement of Motion Study. We are being advised by dentists who have had large European experience and are, consequently, thoroughly familiar with European conditions. We desire to thank them here, and especially to express our appreciation of the coöperation of Dr. J. G. Bunker and Dr. F. L. Marshall for assisting in making Motion Studies. The data derived from such studies will, by means of the Simultaneous Motion Cycle Chart, be adapted to the use of the maimed workers, and the instruction of such workers will be immediately begun. Dental Nursing will then provide a new vocation, and at the same time provide for supplying a community need. It will take no work from those who need it. Rather it will relieve an over-worked profession of low-priced and low-skilled work. Moreover, being based, as it is, on Motion Study and Fatigue Study, it will supply at the same time occupation and interest—those fundamental needs of the crippled in all countries and all times.

MEASUREMENT OF THE HUMAN FACTOR IN INDUSTRY [1]

NO definite and permanent advance is made in any kind of work, whether with materials or men, until use is made of *measurement*. This is especially true of advancement of the human factor in industry, which varies so much that unless we use measurement and abide by the results, there is no possibility of repeating the process accurately and efficiently at will, or of predicting and controlling the future conditions that assure that advancement.

The first step in any great movement is to do exactly what this Society is doing at this Conference —to arouse interest in the subject, to discuss the great problems involved, to outline the possible solutions, and to assign the various problems to those best fitted to undertake and handle them.

The next step is to realize that all this discussion, valuable as it is, can grow into such action as it deserves, only if measurement is insisted upon from

---

[1] Presented at the National Conference of the Western Efficiency Society, May 22-25, 1917.

A ONE-ARMED SIGN-PAINTER WORKING AT HIS FORMER TRADE

Fastening the end of the stick on which he steadies his hand to the shoulder of his coat by means of two rubber bands and two safety-pins, enables him to ply his old trade as well as ever. This device has also been used to advantage by the two-handed worker, as it frees the left hand for the exclusive use of holding the palette.

[*face p* 68

JOBS FOR THE HANDICAPPED

Wholesale chemist's and drug store A one-armed, one-eyed man can operate the cash register, act as cashier, make change, handle the credit file and do up bundles, using the rapid sealing devices instead of twine.

[*face p.* 69

the very beginning of making the investigations outlined; if the records of measurement are in such form that they can be used by those who did not make them, that skill and experience may thus be transferred, and if the results of the measurements are incorporated into actual and universal practice as soon as they are properly synthesized into practical methods of least waste.

The world has come to realize the truth of this as applied to material things. The day of standardization of materials and of machines is far advanced, and is daily progressing; but such has been rarely the case with measurement as applied to the human element.

The design of machines is constantly changing; the human being is constant. Measurement on machines that are obsolete is of little value. Measurement of human beings is valuable forever. Such old saws as "Genius must be unconfined and uncriticized," "Skill is not a matter of measurement or of teaching, but of natural aptitude alone," "Expertness is the same as efficiency and the expert often develops as a lone worker and with no thanks to measurement," have stood in the way of measurement. So have such ideas as that measurement of the human factor, and the supplying of work that this measurement shows to be the most appropriate, lead to monotony.

Now it is a matter of no difficulty to state the facts in their proper terms to an unprejudiced and open mind. Measured investigations prove that genius develops best and fastest when provided with such opportunities as measurement of the genius show as necessary, and when relieved of all restrictive occupation and distraction. They also show that skill *is* largely a matter of training, and that greatest skill can be acquired in the shortest amount of time when right habits are acquired as a direct result of right methods having been taught from the start, and the human factor in the learner and the teacher having been carefully measured.

Most interesting of all, perhaps, is that recent investigations prove absolutely that while expertness and efficiency may be possessed by the same individual, often the expert is not an efficient worker. One of the most expert and most successful orthodontists in the country was proved by motion study measurement to be most wasteful of her motions and of her strength. Many an expert worker in the industries, in the professions and in the sports, shows every evidence of working with speed and with a resulting output high in quality and quantity, but with a resultant fatigue entirely incommensurate with real efficiency. This is no mere theory of ours, not something that we merely base on " what might be" or "what could be," or "what we believe is." It is the actual condition of affairs, as we can prove by records made on recognized experts and champions in numerous lines of activity.

As for the idea that measurement leads, directly or indirectly, to monotony—it has been the direct results of measurement that have proved to be the great factors in eliminating monotony, and in injecting interest into all kinds of work.

Monotony is the result not of measuring the activity, or the human factor in the activity, but of wrong assignment and placement to work, or of such repetition of work that the mind is forced to follow a cycle of activity again and again, with nothing to stimulate during the process. It is the measurement that has resulted in better placement, and in assigning each individual to that type of work for which he will become best fitted, and that he finds interesting. It is the measurement, and the theory and practice of measurement that is taught the individual at the work, that makes him interested in the work itself, in his motions in performing it, and in the rest intervals that enable him to perform the most output with the least fatigue.

How are these measurements made? Thru advances in laboratory psychology, thru educational psychology and thru advances in laboratory practice in the industries, it is now possible to record, accurately and in great detail, not only what the activity is, from the start and over all times, and the paths through which it moves, but also the results. Progress might be greatly accelerated by closer coöperation between workers in various lines all interested in the same problems, though often they fail to realize this fact. Physiologists, psychologists, industrial engineers, managers, and other experts are all interested in so many of the same problems as to astound anyone who understands the various problems, and can compare the investigations in comparative activity now being made. Yet many of the most prominent workers in all these lines, not to speak of the world at large, fail absolutely to realize that the problems being considered *are* common to all and that the results could be of use to the world very much quicker if there was more close coöperation during the period of investigation. Methods and devices could easily be transferred from one type of laboratory to another, findings could be correlated and results classified and utilized to an extent scarcely dreamed of to-day.

As for the methods and devices in use in industrial investigations in particular, we have already presented to you on previous occasions data concerning some of those that we use and have found most helpful. It remains but to say here that these are at the disposal of the nation in this emergency, and have been placed by us already at the national service.

In order to illustrate and to make more concrete the need of measurement in considering the human factor, we bring to you to-day especially, and as one typical example of the whole, the problem of the cripple—the war cripple and the industrial cripple—both of whom constitute elements seriously to be considered in the great problem of preparedness.

Ever since various visits to the warring countries, particularly after the war, and an intensive consideration and study of the problem of the crippled soldier, we have put all possible time, with no remuneration, to the consideration of the problem of re-educating and utilizing the crippled soldier and the crippled worker of the industries.

We realize fully that this is not the time to bring the problem of the war cripples before the youth of the nation in such harrowing form as to prevent enlisting, or in anywise diminish the militant spirit that must exist if our national plans are to be successfully carried through. We realize also, however, that if this country is to succeed better than did the countries abroad in handling this problem, it must be seriously considered *immediately* by such bodies of mature men as this Society. No one realizes more strongly than do the workers in the re-education of the cripples abroad, the need of our nation preparing a Bureau or Department along this line. We had, only a few days ago, a letter from Professor Jules Amar, the great French scientist, who is devoting his time and resources to this work, who has government backing and the most marvelous equipment, and with whom we have been coöperating in crippled soldier work for some time. In this letter Professor Amar urges that this country prepare itself not only along military lines, but along all other lines, for the proper handling of its soldiers. And the French have succeeded in this line with their remarkable ingenuity far beyond any other nation.

We have a well-defined purpose in bringing this subject to the attention of this meeting, which will be brought out plainly at the conclusion of our paper. Let us here outline the things that have happened abroad and in Canada because there has not been sufficient attention paid to measurement of the human factor, and sufficient preparedness to handle the problems that have arisen.

In the first place, there was a universal lack of realization of the great difference existing among the cripples, and of the need of placing each man in that work not only that he was best fitted to do, but that he would most enjoy doing, and that would arouse and hold his interest most successfully and permanently. In the second place, there was a lack of realization of the many more opportunities available for cripples than had been realized. In the third place, there was a lack of realization of the necessity of supplying the proper and fitting re-education for the productive output at the earliest possible moment, in order to bridge over the period of discouragement and despondency, and to help the cripple to fit back into the economic world and its work.

In the fourth place, there was a failure to impress upon the cripple, from the earliest possible moment, his *likeness* to other people and to other workers, rather than his *differences*, and, therefore, as a result, a failure to provide for that *social* element in the work that is necessary, if his permanent happiness is to result. In the fifth place, there was a failure to educate the general community as to what their attitude towards the cripple should be. It is along all these five lines that this preparation must take place, and every one of these lines demands the most accurate measurement of the human factors involved.

First, then, the lack of realization of the difference between individual cripples leads in many instances to teaching them all the same kind of work. This was especially the case where the unfortunate choice was made not of work that was suitable, but of work that was easily taught, or worse yet, work that the available teacher happened to be able to teach. The mistake here was a particularly sad one, in that often this line of work was one that could not possibly appeal to any one of a group of real men who had left real work in the industries or professions to go into the most strenuous of all activities at the front. It was unfortunate, also, that after the cripple had been taught, he was not in a position to look at his new work as a sporting proposition nor to earn an adequate living, nor was he at all satisfied to work permanently at the new work in which he had been most painstakingly taught. For example, many red-blooded men were seriously taught to make baskets, wonderful baskets, that all possible customers could easily go without, that were expected to be sold to people who bought the baskets through pity to help the makers, instead of as a commercial proposition (even our Indians have abandoned basket-making because it is not sufficiently profitable). Most men of the type who have the spirit to fight for their country might be expected to work on baskets so long as they have attractive and interesting teachers, but when taught a trade requiring the variable of charity to be present at a sale of the product, would prefer, in the long run, to drown their sorrows in the standard manner. It must be remembered, then, that it is necessary to find a man's job for these red-blooded individuals, who, with the new opportunities, will be as strenuous in their determination as when they charged the enemies' trenches.

In some cases it is possible to assign a man to work which he has done before he had been injured, and to adapt the working equipment in such a way that he can make a satisfactory output at the work. In many cases it is possible to "re-educate" the man to do a type of work higher than any he has ever done. We have never, as yet, found a case where it was necessary to assign any man to work that could not be made interesting, stimulating and profitable.

The "mental" workers present the simplest problem. The "manual" workers of some education are also easily handled. The difficult element to handle consists of those who have never had the benefit of education—the illiterates. But surprising results have been obtained in all countries, even among this class, where the individual to be placed has been studied with sufficient care. It goes without saying that the nature of the injury or maiming must be most carefully studied also, and that this, along with the study of the mental training, and most especially *the ability to learn*, must be considered in the placement.

Second, as to the lack of realization of opportunities for cripples. In considering the cripple as a subject for placement, we must remember that there are many variables involved. There are the variables of the physical capabilities of the cripple himself, and of the possibilities of supplementing such limbs and faculties as he still possesses with such mechanical devices as are used so successfully by Professor Amar. The most rapid survey of the illustrations of any of the several wonderful accounts of the work being done by him, show that he has carried mechanical adaptation and supplementing of the capacities of the cripple to a truly marvelous extent.

Another variable is the amount of adaptation possible with the working equipment that the cripple is to use. We have already given an account of the possibilities of adapting the typewriter through the use of a double keyboard, of a supply of paper from continuous multiple rolls and other devices furnished us by the Remington, the Monarch and the Smith Premier Typewriter Companies, to the use of the crippled typist. Another variable is the possibility of re-education, mental and manual, of the cripple himself. Along with existing, realized and unrealized, opportunities for the cripple are others that result from the creation of lines of activity not yet existing, but much needed for the community good, such as that of Dental Nursing. This we have already described,[1] and need only say here that it consists of taking from the unfunctionalized over-burdened profession of Dentistry the routine work of cleaning the teeth, and assigning this to properly trained and inspected cripples, who will, under State Supervision and after the instruction of experts, supplement the work of the dentist, add to the health and well-being of the community, and at the same time furnish dental prophylaxis at a price that the poor family can afford.

It is along this line that we make our first plea to you for coöperation in finding jobs specially adapted to cripples. In your own particular occupation, no matter what it is, there undoubtedly exist opportunities for cripples, both discovered and undiscovered, and it is a part of your duty to your nation, and of your contribution to adequate preparedness, that you yourself discover these opportunities, record

---

[1] "The Conservation of the World's Teeth. A New Occupation for Crippled Soldiers," Conference Society for the Promotion of Occupational Therapy, March, 1917. See *ante*.

them and present them for national consideration. If you have a successful cripple in your employ, if you know a cripple who is a productive member of the community, his occupation must be one suitable for some other man crippled similarly, and it is your duty to record all existing data as fully as possible along such lines, noting particularly how he has achieved economic and industrial success, that others may be cheered and encouraged particularly during their transition periods. If you note in your observation of your own activity, or your own line of work, *any* places that could be filled by cripples of any possible type, it is your duty to record these also.

Of course, with the Simultaneous Motion Cycle Chart it is possible to take almost any line of activity and study it and adapt it in such a way as to place a crippled worker at least a part of the activity. But there is one way in which your observations will have more value than will those made through the laboratory methods, *i.e.*, the great immediate need of the man who has been crippled, after he has been made physically comfortable, is for encouragement and comfort. This can be obtained quickest through accounts of actual existing men who have suffered similar injuries and who have made good. If you will record these for his use in the most simple and elementary fashion, the human element there will at once make itself felt in the encouragement and heartening of the newly-made cripple.

Third, you must realize the great need of supplying this incentive to live and this re-education at the *earliest possible moment.* Mr. George E. Barton, Director of the Consolation House in Clifton Springs, New York, who has had a long, most interesting and valuable experience with cripples, with maimed, and with convalescents of all kinds, agrees with us that the crucial period is at the earliest possible moment in the convalescence.[1] With the war cripples a serious complication occurs here if this stimulus is not at once supplied. In the case of those of much education and training, if there is no stimulus at this time, despair and direful consequences are more than apt to occur. If the man has not much education or constructive imagination, and the period of re-education is postponed—between the money that he receives without effort, and the misdirected sympathy of his friends, he is apt to fall into habits of idleness, if not worse, that are extremely difficult to overcome later. This is universally acknowledged by those both abroad and in this country who have worked with cripples.

Speaking of the money, or the pensions, it must

---

[1] See papers by George Edward Barton, Clifton Springs, New York.

be understood that nothing that we say in any way contemplates doing away with pensions. We agree with all those who sympathize with the cripples that they deserve—having " done their bit "—the thanks and reward of their country, and an opportunity to rest, if they so desire and if this is possible. However, the majority of them do *not* desire to remain idle, and it is necessary, for their own good as well as the good of the country, that they be allowed to supplement these pensions by all that they can earn and yet remain physically and mentally at their best.

It is necessary at this time to realize, also, that ability to supply this need when it arises depends largely upon our being prepared well in advance of the immediate need. On returning from two trips abroad after an extensive study of conditions there, and strenuously advocating general preparedness for our nation, we were laughed at as mad and foolish for thinking that this country would be involved in the great tumult abroad. Now, when we again advocate as warmly and as persistently preparing for this crippled soldier problem, we are again told, even in Washington, that we are " in advance of the times " and that " there is no need for haste in this matter." We wish to impress upon this Society most strongly, at this particular point, the need, if we are to conserve the best there is in our returning men, mentally and physically, of preparing for their reception and their re-education at once.

To consider fourth the need for a social element in the work. Too much of the work assigned to and taught to cripples carries the inference that they will work either as " lone workers," in their homes, or in communities of cripples like themselves. Now, we all know there is no punishment like ostracism, there is nothing that troubles the average human being like being considered different from his fellows. We must make the cripple feel, from the earliest possible moment, that, in essentials, he is like every other member of the community, and that the quicker he " fits back " into the social and industrial life of the community, the better for the community as well as for his own self.

It is, therefore, with particular pleasure that we see some of the newer opportunities for cripples that are being discovered. We are glad to acknowledge here the hearty coöperation of the National Cash Register Company in discovering and recording such opportunities. There are opportunities in stores, opportunities for handling vending machines, for selling tobacco, papers, periodicals, candy, souvenir postcards ; for tending and operating telephones and telegraphs, telautographs, cash registers, credit files, dictaphones and circulating libraries ; opportunities for selling-booths in hotel corridors; opportunities in small stores, and as ticket sellers and choppers in subway stations. When you realize what these opportunities are, and the broad field in which they lie, you will discover numerous opportunities in your own organizations, and can coöperate and assist us in bringing these to national attention. The great benefit of all of these opportunities is that utilizing them for cripples will not only free people for other lines of activity that demand "whole" workers, but that the cripples will enjoy social life as well as opportunities for productive work for the community.

Of course some suggested occupations will require the usual changes or adaptations. For example, an elevator operator's job requires no legs if the man be supplied with a stool. This is perfectly practicable in this country, where there are no such ceremonies on entering and leaving a lift as exist abroad.

This leads us naturally to the fifth topic, the need of educating the public. Whenever we suggest a line of work—for example, Dental Nursing—as well adapted to the work of cripples, we are sure to hear the objection that "the public does not wish to be brought into such close contact with the cripple." It "will never stand for that." Now the public must be educated, at the earliest possible moment,

JOBS FOR THE HANDICAPPED

The proper analysis of work will permit judicious placement of the crippled so that they will not be handicapped at all in their duties. The examination of the Simultaneous Motion Cycle Charts with reference to the limbs and faculties missing or injured as compared with the requirements for doing a certain kind of work, will reveal that the cripple can perform his duties just as efficiently as the normal worker. This picture shows a department for telephone orders, a credit file, cash register, and bins for small parts of stock.

[face p 84

Small Stores for the Handicapped

This small store is located near the entrance of a building. The operator acts as an information bureau; sells small office supplies; operates a long-distance and interior telephone and utilizes his periods of unavoidable delay transcribing from a dictating machine. He serves many of the tenants in the building by recording inward messages and by carrying out their orders over the telephone, which have been dictated to him on a cylinder, and by helping out on typing when their typists are rushed or are away on vacations The possibilities of the dictating machines have never been properly utilized on cripple work, and whether or not a crippled typist has learned stenography, a couple of extra dictating machines loaned by him to tenants not already possessing them is one of the most profitable things with which a cripple can be furnished. A dictating outfit is one of the most efficient devices for utilizing *all* of a cripple's spare time.

to the realization that the cripple is already an unrecognized large portion of the community, as can be easily realized by noting the large number of factories devoted exclusively to the manufacture of artificial limbs, and is destined to become a larger portion, as long as the war lasts and even after that, until we do away, as is possible to a greater extent, with industrial accidents. It is this feeling toward the cripple, which probably started in natural sympathy, and a desire to spare the cripple activity, that has resulted in making the average cripple feel that he is different from the other members of the community, and estranged from them; and it is this feeling that we must combat at the earliest and at every possible opportunity.

The pity for the cripple under the proper system of education should be supplemented by great admiration for the courage and expertness of the cripple, and by a desire to coöperate in making him a productive and a more satisfied member of the community. Again, the public must be educated as to the necessity of providing a definite livelihood for the cripple. It is not enough that we give the cripple a *chance* to earn a living, we must be sure that he *gets* the living. It is not enough to give him a "fair chance with other competitors," for he may not have been trained to meet the lifelong training of unhandicapped experts. It will be especially easy to emphasize the possibilities of giving and insuring this living to the cripples who are placed in these new types of little stores. This can be done, first, by sending the customers to him; next, by notifying all possible customers *who* and *where* he is—the "where" being taken care of by special signs on the street, such as druggists' signs in certain countries abroad; third, by notifying customers *what* he is; fourth, by providing such state or community controlled societies acting as jobbers for cripples who are comparatively small buyers who can handle small orders for the cripple, handle credits and take away the voucher of "deserving cripple in good standing," or "military cripple in good standing." These jobbers will afford us an opportunity of guiding the distribution, purchasing and selling expense of those who are handicapped as original producers, and help to turn the necessary unproductive expense due to distribution marketing and service over to those who are handicapped.

Again, the public must be educated to a feeling that after certain jobs have been designated as suitable for cripples they should, as soon as there are cripples to fill them, be reserved for these cripples. It should become at least "not fashionable" to do any work that can be done by a maimed man, nor to employ a whole worker in a job that can be properly handled by a cripple out of employment.

This readjustment is no new thing, nor is it one demanded only by the situation with regard to cripples. We have for years advocated the reclassification of the trades. This reclassification has always been needed. It happens that this new element in the problem, or rather the increased importance of this element at this time, makes the need for such reclassification and reassignment all the more important.

These, then, are the various factors of the cripple problem as they exemplify the need for measurement of the human factor, and we bring them before this Society at this time because your coöperation is so necessary. Experts as you are, each in his particular line, each of you is making at this time a fight for measurement, for standardization, and for adequate preparedness. We urge you not only to continue this good fight, and to advocate that measurement be applied to all lines, but we urge you to consider this necessity of measurement as applied to the placement of the cripple as an excellent starting point.

The war cripple holds human interest to-day, anything that has to do with him grips the sympathies, and where the sympathies are once aroused results will certainly follow, if we but persevere sufficiently. Now, there are two by-products to this, each of which is greater than the aforestated direct product.

1. The industrial cripples are much more numerous than the war cripples. This has always been so, and is true even in Canada to-day. Let us therefore take advantage of the present interest and enthusiasm to handle the problem of the industrial cripple whom we will have with us always.

2. The study of the special problems of the cripple, his capabilities for highest placement and success, his special and motion study education and guidance are better adapted to solve the problems of vocational guidance, placement, education and individual efficiency of the youth and workers of our country than all other known sources combined. This is particularly well shown by the fact that each of the successful studies that we have completed to enable the crippled to compete with the unmaimed has resulted in information or apparatus or less wasteful motions that have also been correspondingly useful and valuable for the unmaimed.

In other words, the cripple's needs are immediate. In serving him we are at the same time collecting the most valuable motion study data, and data relating to educational and industrial methods of least waste.

Small Stores for the Handicapped

The handicapped can often make a good living by having small stores, selling such things as newspapers and periodicals, and operating circulating libraries. In some cases they have been allowed to have small stores of their own while operating as cashiers for employers. A census of opportunities for door-men and such to also have small stores of their own to operate during their periods of "unavoidable delay" reveals countless opportunities for the handicapped to utilize *all* of their time to advantage.

Jobs for the Handicapped

Switchboards, credit files, cash registers, outward and inside telephones. What is needed is surveys for proper jobs for the handicapped by the employers. They can earn a living if the managers and employers use sufficient intelligence For particularly good methods for making such surveys, see those devised by Mr. A. B Segur, Red Cross Institute for the Blind, under the Surgeon General's Dept., Baltimore, Maryland, U.S.A.

This is a national need that one can realize better after talking with a keen observer who has recently returned from foreign travel, particularly from the Far East.

Will you not therefore, in your consideration for, and in your work along the lines of the Human Factor in Industrial Preparedness, and in your advocacy of measurement along these lines, consider in your own particular work the military and industrial cripples, present and future, who need the results of this work so sorely, and coöperate, not only in finding opportunities for the individual, but in educating the great public with whom you come in contact as to the needs, and also to the remedies for these needs? By so doing you will add to the productivity and wealth of our country and to the great sum total of the happiness minutes which are the ultimate units that we all aim to produce.

THE ENGINEER, THE CRIPPLE AND THE NEW EDUCATION [1]

This paper is a progress report and states definitely the work that the engineer should do to help the cripple to be independent of all charity. It states how the cripple can be enabled to compete successfully with normal workers in the trades at the present time. It calls attention to the fact that the cripple after receiving intensive education by means of micromotion study is able to earn more than normal workers who have not received such education.

The war has made an upheaval in many methods, particularly those of education. After the war the intensive methods now used in our emergency will be used permanently. These methods are not transitory. They will remain because they are more efficient.

The intensive education in motion study, of the one best way to do work now being done for the cripple, is the model for all the intensive training of the nation's workers after peace comes—that they are more efficient, more productive and less fatigued, The military cripple will thus have served his country doubly.

THE purpose of this paper is to report progress in the solution of the problem of training the crippled soldier. At the present stage of this work we are able to formulate certain conclusions that have a bearing upon the activities of

[1] Presented at the Annual Meeting, December, 1917, of The American Society of Mechanical Engineers, New York.

this Society and upon the part that the Engineer should take in the Crippled Soldier work.

2. These conclusions are as follows:

a. The Crippled Soldier problem is practically identical to the problem of the cripple in general.

b. Its solution lies in a new type of education.

c. This education is destined to be the education of the future.

d. It is based on

(1) Finding the ONE BEST WAY TO DO WORK.

(2) Adequate assignment to work, *i.e.*, intensive vocational guidance.

e. The engineer is best fitted to determine the one best way, to formulate it into methods, and to supply necessary devices and mechanical appliances.

3. All cripples, no matter what the cause of the crippling, require a training that will be mentally satisfying and physically beneficial. This training must be such as will enable them to become productive members of the community, and to remain on the world's pay roll. This implies either competing with non-crippled workers in occupations open to all, or setting aside certain work for crippled workers exclusively, or both. It implies discovering

and making available such opportunities for crippled workers, discovering which cripple is best fitted to utilize the opportunity, and training him to make the best possible use of it. It also implies not only opportunities for individual development, but such social opportunities as will enable the cripple to fit back into the ordinary social life with the ease and the largest amount of durable greatest satisfaction.

4. Those crippled in war furnish a small percentage of the total crippled as compared with those crippled from other causes, such as disease and accidents, especially in the industries. This is true even in Canada, which has furnished such a remarkable quota of fighting men in comparison with the total number of her population.

5. The solution of the crippled-soldier problem as outlined above consists of a type of education that is *new*, in that it eliminates the greatest amount of waste possible in the educational process. It teaches *the one best way* at the outset, instead of following the old practice of "learn every way," with the vague hope of arriving at efficiency as an outcome. It enables the learner to arrive at a desired outcome with the greatest amount of speed and the least amount of effort, and with the largest return in efficiency and the resulting satisfaction.

6. Because of these qualities, this new education is bound to be used in the future not only in the re-education of cripples in what is to be their new life work, but in education in general. Just as the Montessori method of teaching children, which originated in an effort to discover the best method of training subnormals, proved so successful in that field and demonstrated such underlying principles of general applicability that it now occupies an important place in the training of normal and supernormal children, so this new method of education, discovered as a result of synthesizing measurements of champion workers in our *quest of the one best way to do work,* is spreading through the general interest in re-educating military cripples to the re-education of all cripples, into the manual-training schools, corporation schools and the general educational fields.

7. The new education has two parts: first, discovering the one best way to do work, and second, testing the individual and placing him at the demonstrated most appropriate work. By " work " we mean activity of any kind, whether physical or mental, for the investigations and the resulting methods are being made and applied in mental as well as physical fields of activity, as a result of our findings based on micromotion and cyclegraph

records which prove that the laws of habit formation apply equally well to mental and motion work.

8. There should be little argument as to the desirability of finding the one best way to do anything, regardless of whether it is immediately learned, taught or habitually practised. There has been considerable discussion as to the possibility of there being any one best way, and also as to the possibility of finding it, if it does exist. The important thing is that there certainly is one best *available* way. There is no question of this, since it has been demonstrated both in theory and in practice. This way seldom if ever exists in the consecutive motion-cycle units of any one individual, though their units may be in general use, and many will undoubtedly be used by every expert in the activity.

9. Of the matter of tests and assignment and placement at most appropriate work, we need only say here that the discovery of the one best way of doing the work and the consequent standardization of the best methods and equipment will allow of tests that are more adequate. For this reason, if we can test the proposed worker with the method and device that it is planned he shall use, we shall have less variables in our testing process than is the case at present, and we shall have less difficulty

in the evaluation of the tests, and less necessary transfer.

10. The engineer is the natural person to whom the world now looks to find *the one best way.* This one best way is based on accurate measurement—not guesswork, personal opinion, bias, or the vote of a majority of a committee who have not measured. The engineer's training in measurement fits him specially for doing the requisite work.

11. To recapitulate, the *extent* of the cripple problem is, then, practically unlimited. When we come to consider the subject closely we see that every one of us is in some degree a cripple, either through being actually maimed or through having some power or faculty which has not been developed or used to its fullest extent. The degree of crippling extends from the worker who, through some accident, has lost his eyesight, his hearing, and the use of his legs, arms and hands except for the use of one finger—and by the way this is no imaginary illustration, as we have lately received a skillfully woven bag made by such a cripple maimed through a mining accident—to a man who is dependent upon glasses for reading. From an efficiency standpoint a policeman with corns on the soles of his feet or a golfer with the gout in his toe is more of a cripple during his working hours than a legless man while operating on

a typewriter. We can, then, think of every member of the community as having been a cripple, as being a cripple, or as a potential cripple. Conversely, we can think of a badly mutilated man as not being a cripple during the period that he is at that work *the performance of which is not affected by the mutilation.*

12. As to the *nature* of the problem of the cripple, it is a problem of education, as has been said. *With the present state of the art of teaching it is largely a problem of re-education,* since most of us, non-crippled as well as crippled, have received the wrong type of education and must be re-educated even in the fundamentals. As an example of the inefficient method of education, consider the practice of having foreign languages taught exclusively by teachers speaking dialects or worse, instead of by supplementing the best available teaching by talking-machine records of the experts in pronunciation. As education becomes more scientific the problems of re-education will become simplified, and the process will become shortened.

13. As to the natural solvers of the problem of the crippled soldier, these are, as before stated, the engineers, but only if the engineers will bring to the task the scientific attitude. As a profession we have been too apt to be satisfied with half-way methods and half-way devices. We boast of the advance in

engineering science, especially of the advances in the science of management, which have to date been, with few exceptions, the work of engineers, yet general knowledge and use of instruments of precision, even when such are available, are lamentably lacking. As a specific example of this we may cite the use of the stop watch by experienced and earnest investigators in the field of time study. If the engineer, knowing as he must that it is an insurmountable barrier to obtaining *the best method,* or even knowledge of times that are transferable to others, is to discover *the one best way to do work* he must use the best methods and instruments extant, and he must apply these with unremitting accuracy, persistence and patience. *The one best way* consists of elements of motions accurately timed and recorded, and synthesized into the best available method of activity.

14. If the engineers are, as a profession, ever to take the place that they should take in this work they must start *now* to coöperate with those working in other phases of the subject. The various aspects of the problem are being assigned to those best able to handle them. For example, the task of making surveys as to what should be and is being done and of the opportunities open to cripples can well be undertaken by cities, towns and other civic organiza-

tions. This is being done, notably in Chicago, where we are assisting in the excellent work now under way under the leadership of Mr. Pike, Mr. Petterson and others. The matter of furnishing money for the investigations and for the work itself is being excellently attended to by the Red Cross, as, for example, through the Red Cross Institute, New York City, with which we are coöperating, which has sent Dr. Edward Devine abroad for personal investigation and service in the field. There is also the work of Mr. McMurtrie, Acting Director of this Institute, who is collecting a bibliography on the subject of cripples. The matter of investigating the extent of the crippling and of providing the surgical and medical attention necessary is being admirably handled under the able leadership of the Surgeon-General and other Government representatives, already famous in the medical and surgical profession, in Washington. Too much credit cannot be given to Dr. Franklin Martin and Surgeon-General Gorgas for the progress that they have made in this great work in the short time since the day after the declaration of war, when they individually honored one of the writers by giving him an interview for the purpose of outlining possible work along these lines, since which time he has been honored by being appointed on Dr. Martin's committee reporting to the Council of Defense, and is now also coöperating with Col. Owen and other famous doctors in the Surgeon-General's department.

15. The psychologists have appointed committees to investigate all branches of the subject that come within their field. The psychotherapists are working on their aspect of the problem, and Mr. George Edward Barton, of the Consolation House at Clifton Springs, Past-President of the National Society for the Promotion of Occupational Therapy, has spent years in theoretical and practical work concerning the convalescence period, and is contributing his experience and energies toward helping this cause. Educators are considering not only the training of the necessary teachers but the training of the cripples themselves, notably Prof. Frank E. Sanborn of Ohio State University and Prof. Wm. S. Ayars of Nova Scotia Technical College, an American engaged for years in teaching in Canada, both of whom are members of this Society.

16. A Government bureau for collecting and conserving all this data will come naturally as a development of the activity in other fields and of the present activity of various Government departments along various lines. This bureau should contain a museum that would include among its exhibits models of artificial limbs and appliances for

cripples. This, supplemented by state and municipal museums along similar lines, would bring first-hand knowledge to the cripple, who too often buys the first artificial limb he sees, and usually averages three or four purchases before he gets the one best suited to him.

17. Such a national museum should also contain fatigue-eliminating devices, which would enable all workers to become more productive with less accompanying fatigue. The writers first called the attention of this Society to this need in 1910, feeling that fatigue study, like accident prevention, is a function of the engineer. We have, since 1913, started several small museums of devices for eliminating unnecessary fatigue, hoping that the movement would spread, and in the winter of 1915 tried to get the National Museum at Washington to start such a department, but apparently were not able to arouse much interest, though we were asked and thanked for a collection of wire models of motions. Recently Col. Owen became interested, and now a definite start has been made.

18. The great need for fatigue elimination for the crippled soldier will undoubtedly lead to interest in the subject in this country as it has in England, for until recently we have had much more encouragement in our campaign for fatigue study from Englishmen than from our own countrymen. Mr. James F.

Butterworth, ever ready to disseminate information relating to managerial economics, was the first to bring the matter to the attention of the British public. Prof. A. F. Stanley Kent incorporated his investigations of fatigue of munitions workers into Reports, written by order of the King, since reprinted by this Government and obtainable at Washington. Prof. Henry J. Spooner wrote a series of articles on Industrial Fatigue in its Relation to Maximum Output for *Co-Partnership* (London), since issued as a booklet, which should be in the hands of every engineer and employer, and should also be reprinted by our Government and put on sale by the Superintendent of Documents.

19. The data for such reports and articles come from investigations of present conditions, and realization of their significance. If the present chairs and work benches now to be found in all parts of this country as well as abroad were collected and put beside such efficient devices as the Barney chair and foot rest, and the Marshall travelling chair, they would look as out of place and cruel as do the devices of torture of the medieval period. Observing this, and with the cripple in mind, it will be noted that the principles underlying the adapting of chairs and foot rests to the industrial worker's measurements and to the needs of the cripple are identical. If this

had been realized more generally sooner, more people would have taken up fatigue study and the devising of chairs, foot rests and benches to meet the national after-the-war need for more efficient working conditions for cripple and non-cripple alike.

20. This profession as a whole has not given the full benefits of its education, training and ingenuity to the industrial cripples of the past. The more we investigate the problem of the cripple the more we marvel at their patience and the fortitude with which their calamities have been met and endured. They have made so few demands. They have been so pitifully eager to coöperate in this new work. They are, throughout the entire country, for the first time seeing the opportunity to do constructive work for their fellows, not only by showing what the maimed and handicapped can do but by acting as examples of cheerfulness and continuity of purpose for all to follow. They are seizing this chance to do their bit for the war and for their country, and have shown such intelligent coöperation that we are led to agree with Mr. Fred J. Miller, Past Vice-President of this Society, that a man who has lost a limb becomes thereafter more active both physically and mentally.

21. Now the needs of our industrial cripples are

supplemented by the more pressing need of the crippled soldiers. The crippled soldier is at a disadvantage, as compared with the industrial cripple, in that he is often at a distance from aid of various kinds at the time that the crippling takes place, and thus misses the chance for the early re-education that is desirable and necessary. Second, in that through mistaken kindness he is not taught work of any kind during his convalescence and during the period immediately after his return home; in fact, he is often encouraged by misguided friends to remain idle until the possibility of teaching the maimed member and the mind that has stopped learning has decreased, and re-education becomes more difficult, if not actually impossible. Third, through the terrible physical and mental anguish that often precedes as well as follows the crippling.

22. The crippled soldier has the advantage over the industrial cripple in that he is the object of great interest and patriotic sympathy, therefore is a member of the community to be courted rather than shunned; in that he suffers in the limelight, and therefore is practically assured of assistance as soon as the world is convinced as to what he needs; in that he will have, if he has not now, expert training at his disposal; in that he has the consolation of fame and of having done something worth while, even

though he had to pay the penalty of being crippled for having done it.

23. For these reasons it is advisable that the engineer turn his attention immediately to the problem of the crippled soldier, supplying the new education in the form of re-education for this soldier, with the assurance that when the methods and devices have been supplied the industrial and other cripples will benefit exactly as will the crippled soldier.

24. We have already brought out, in papers on progress in crippled-soldier work, the various needs that must be met. One is the need of adapting methods and devices to the cripple, and another the need of adapting the cripple to existing methods and devices. The engineer has a part in meeting both these needs, that is :

a. In inventing or adapting detached devices that will make it possible for cripples to do various kinds of work, such as various devices furnished us by the makers of the Remington, Monarch and Smith Premier typewriters, that enabled a one-eyed, legless, one-armed and one-fingered typist to write many more short letters in a given time than can the unmaimed champion typist of the world.

b. In providing artificial limbs to replace those missing. Particular attention is called to the possibilities of inventing countless designs of articulated limbs controlled by systematized use of the trunk muscles controlling the joints of the limbs by means of wires and springs for replacing other muscles and tendons.

c. In inventing or adapting devices that may be attached to the cripple himself, not to replace missing limbs, but in effect to supply new ones, *i.e.*, additional limbs that will enable him to use existing equipment and thus accomplish work.

25. Artificial limbs may therefore be supplemented or supplanted by what we have called "supplementary limbs," for examples, (1) a ring or loop attached to the suspenders or belt for assisting a one-armed man to handle a shovel, as suggested and used practically by Dean Cullamore of Delaware University; (2) yokes, special belts and grasping devices operated by pressure of the body against the work bench; (3) "the third thumb" for holding a magnifying glass.

26. Undoubtedly for all-around and general purposes it would seem to many people presumptuous to attempt to improve much upon nature in the

question of the design of the human being. There is a resemblance here to our educational systems. Our educational systems are extremely good in many cases for all-around purposes, but they can be easily improved upon by anyone who knows exactly what is needed for a special case. We therefore urge all who undertake this work of specially fitting the cripple to perform an activity not to hesitate to "improve on nature" at any time. This new viewpoint will help to handle many difficult cases. We hope soon to present a paper showing in detail practice of putting an extra number of limbs at the disposal of the unmaimed worker, a development of this work for cripples.

27. We have been much assisted in adapting both devices and cripples by the use of our Simultaneous Cycle Motion Chart. Through the elements there listed, such as "search," "find," "select," "grasp" and "transport" we have been enabled to invent or suggest, in highly repetitive work, some contrivances that are creating a new era in efficiency, as can be easily realized when the comparative simultaneous cycle motion charts before and after the investigation are studied. It is but necessary to call attention to the facts that all "grasping" is not done by the hand; that "positioning" may even be a function of the mouth; that the ordinary workman's

apron with its many pockets may be used to relieve working members of the body, and that " inspection " for quantity and quality is by no means always a function of the eyes. There is an opportunity in " the device to handle the device " that will satisfy the yearnings of the most ambitious mechanical and inventive mind, a field almost without end that will eventually make the new era in industry date from the sacrifices of this war. The accompanying pictures show some of the devices and methods already in use, and are valuable simply as suggestions as to what can be done along these lines.

28. We could supplement this plea to the engineering profession to enter into this work as a professional duty, *i.e.*, as service, by an appeal to your sympathies that would bring you into the work with a rush. No one who has not seen with his own eyes the pitiful condition of those who come out of the trenches dazed and forlorn, worse off mentally than physically because of shattered nerves, anxious as to the future, and with a feeling of general unfitness to " fit back " into every-day activity, can realize the pressing need for re-education and for placement. Next to seeing all this is the reading of the wonderful books of the genius Amar,[1]

[1] *The Human Motor*, translated by E. P. Butterworth (Routledge), and *The Physiology of Industrial Organization* The Library Press).

and the study of the illustrations—actual photographs of workers equipped with his marvelous articulated limbs, and accounts of the training being furnished in France, at the hospitals and in the re-education schools, through the work of Amar and those coöperating with him.[1] Add to these the reading of other books, and better yet of personal letters from those in England or Canada who have seen or worked with the cripples who returned before re-education was definitely attempted, and who, because of lack of immediate training, slipped into idleness and worse. The importance of habits of work must always be kept in mind.[2] This fact has been emphasized by Past-President Hartness in the first two chapters of "The Human Factor in Works Management," and by Mr. Henry L. Gantt, Past Vice-President, in various papers read before this Society, and in Chapter VIII of "Work, Wages and Profits." It is this need for conserving or forming right habits of work that makes immediate action imperative.

29. For Humanity's sake, for our own sake we, as a profession, must go into this crippled-soldier work. There has been much talk of late years of

---

[1] "To Prepare Soldier Cripples for Industry," *The Iron Age*, October 25, 1917.

[2] See "The Psychology of Management," MacMillan & Co., New York.

" the human element," and of the engineer's neglect of consideration of it. The engineer is certainly doing his bit in the war work with material things. This crippled-soldier work is the human-element side.

30. For those who have hungered for religious opportunities, here is the chance. For those who are preaching " Good will on earth," " Love your neighbor," and " As ye would that men should do do you, do ye also to them likewise," here is the big opportunity, and it is at hand—on every hand. The chance to help our fellow-man—the military cripple, the non-military cripple, in fact all of the nation's workers. The chance to push forward the new learning, the method of attack for obtaining the one best way. The greatest patriotic opportunity to make the entire nation more prosperous !

31. Let us take the three phrases—the Engineer, the Cripple, the New Education—and by our activity in the Crippled Soldier work relate these three so closely with one another that through the engineer's participation in the new education the cripple may be transformed from a " discard " to a " champion," who has won personal success in spite of a handicap, and who has used his individual variation from normal to foster the national movement of better methods of education.

THE CRIPPLED SOLDIER IN INDUSTRY [1]

THE problem of the crippled soldier in industry is not a problem of war work only; it is a problem of industrial development. As individuals, each one of you is seeking to provide our maimed heroes with such teaching as will render them, in the shortest possible amount of time, productive and satisfied members of the community. As individuals you are interested in the organizations that are preparing to receive these men, to train them and to place them at that work for which they are best fitted.

As an organization, it is now your duty to take up the industrial end of the problem, to investigate existing conditions in the industries, to discover where the opportunities for employment lie, and so readjust industrial practice that the cripples may be utilized to their own and the community's good with the least shock to themselves or to the industries, and with the greatest amount of permanent benefit to all concerned.

---

[1] Presented at the New York Meeting, February, 1918, of the American Institute of Mining Engineers.

We have divided industrial opportunities suitable for cripples, roughly, into three classes. *First*, such as already exist in the industries, which can be set aside for cripples only, present occupants being transferred to other work for which they can be fitted but which is not suitable for cripple work; *second*, opportunities in the industrial world that, through changes in the working equipment or tools, or through appliances attached to the cripple himself, can make the cripple a competitor of the sound worker; *third*, opportunities not existing at present in the industries, but which could be introduced for the good of the community, without placing the cripples into competition with any existing class of workers.

As typical of the first type of occupations for cripples, we have mentioned that of store-keeper, of the second type that of typist [1] and of the third type that of dental nurse.[2] The last occupation can be so arranged as to take from the overworked dentist the work of cleaning teeth; and after careful investigation and embodiment of the resulting data into standards, teaching can be provided that will enable the cripple to perform this work satisfactorily and profitably. In a session held at the recent

[1] "How to Put the Crippled Soldier on the Pay Roll." *The Trained Nurse and Hospital Review* (May, 1917). See *ante*.

[2] "Conservation of the World's Teeth." *The Trained Nurse and Hospital Review* (July, 1917). See *ante*.

annual meeting of the American Society of Mechanical Engineers for the discussion of the crippled soldier problem from all aspects, we emphasized the fact that it is the duty of the engineer to provide the new education for the cripples, that is to say, to investigate by careful measurement methods of doing work, and to formulate the One Best Way by which each type of activity should be performed.[1] By this means it is possible to eliminate waste in the teaching and learning process, and to enable the crippled soldier to get upon the pay-roll most quickly and most profitably.

Supplementing this duty of the engineer is a second duty, which is to investigate the industry to which he belongs in the most thorough fashion and to note the existence, or the possibility, of the three types of industrial opportunity mentioned, in order that the properly trained crippled soldier may be placed with the least amount of delay possible. The training is already insured, for not only are the foremost minds in re-education in this country in all lines of activity interested, but the great scientists abroad have offered coöperation and actual training in their schools and laboratories ; notably Prof. Jules Amar, whose masterly work in re-education is soon to be presented to us in English.

[1] "The Engineer, the Cripple and the New Education." *Journal, American Society of Mechanical Engineers* (1918), 40, 51.

It remains now to provide the work for the re-educated. Much is already being done by state and national departments, by cities and by trade organizations, but it is essential that the engineer, working as he does in many industries, start *at once* to make a survey that is scientific.

There are several methods by which this side of the problem may be attacked. *First*, by making careful records of all cripples at present employed in the industries, of the nature of the crippling, of the type of devices in use to enable the cripple to perform his work satisfactorily, of the type of the training found adequate, of the records made by these men and of any recommendations as to the use of that type of work for future cripples. *Second*, by making a Fatigue Survey [1] in every industry, that will record all fatigue-eliminating methods and devices, since these can often be easily adapted so as to make the occupation a possible one for a cripple. *Third*, by studying all machinery and equipment in use in the industries, with the idea of inventing appliances which will enable the same to be operated by a crippled worker. *Fourth*, by classifying all occupations in the industries according to the particular faculties demanded. That is to say, listing under

[1] "Fatigue Study," chap. II. New York, Macmillan & Co., 1916.

one head all those requiring keen eyesight, under another head all those requiring keen hearing, and under a third all those where a fine sense of touch is essential, etc. Through such a classification alone, many possible occupations for maimed and crippled have been discovered. *Fifth,* by classifying all occupations according to the amount of endurance or strength required. This classification of occupations should be made before women workers are introduced into an industry where they have not worked before, and many of the investigations necessary for placing the cripples can be much curtailed if the crippled-soldier problem, the problem of introducing women into the industries and the fatigue-elimination problem are all considered at the same time, since they involve many common elements.

Another method of investigating the industries for opportunities is according to the *elements of motions* involved in the activity. Every motion may be divided into at least sixteen elements. These are: (1) Search; (2) Find; (3) Select; (4) Grasp; (5) Position; (6) Transport, loaded; (7) Assemble; (8) Use; (9) Dissemble, or take apart; (10) Inspect; (11) Position for next operation; (12) Release load; (13) Transport, empty; (14) Wait (unavoidable delay; (15) Wait (avoidable delay); (16) Rest (for overcoming fatigue). The scientific method of studying these elements of a motion consists of recording the path of the motion through the micromotion method and the cyclegraph method, and then arraying the resulting data on the Simultaneous Motion Cycle Chart, called "Motion Chart" for brevity.[1] Through this method an exact record of the path of the motion and of the time consumed by the motion is made, and one is enabled, through the charting, to visualize the parts of the body that are acting simultaneously and what each part of the body does during the entire motion cycle. It is obvious that from this information it is possible to transfer activity from one member of the body to another, to supply equipment that will make it possible to utilize different limbs from those previously used, to eliminate useless motions or substitute more efficient ones, and, ultimately, to use the results for the selection of that type of worker best fitted to do the work according to the ultimate standard method, for placement and for teaching.

But for survey purposes it is possible to observe an activity without instruments of precision and to make some rough estimates as to how suitable it is for a cripple occupation. For example, take the first element, "Search." In many an existing operation

---

[1] "Motion Study for the Crippled Soldier." *Journal, American Society of Mechanical Engineers* (1915), **37**, 669. See *ante*.

to-day the searching is done both with the hand and with the eye. This is reduplication of effort, and your Secretary, Mr. Stoughton, can doubtless tell you of the wonderful work that has been done with the blind in making "Search" (1), "Find" (2), "Select" (3), and "Grasp" (4) into one operation. In applying the results of motion study in the industries, it has been possible to make this same combination through the use of cross-sectioning, and through placing materials on a fixed spot, in the proper position to be grasped. Again, through the packet method, which provides for the arrangement of materials on a proper support and in the required sequence and the proper position to be transported to the next operation, it is possible to combine "Search" (1), "Find" (2), "Select" (3), "Grasp" (4) and "Position" (5), and to make of the entire five elements one operation requiring nothing but a simultaneous reach and grasp. The elements "Assemble" (7), "Use" (8), and "Dissemble" (9) can also, in many cases, be performed without the use of the eyes and with the effort involved much minimized through the use of proper desks and work-benches, chairs, arm-rests and foot-rests. An enormous amount of fatigue can be removed on many types of operations if the forearms are properly supported. This is the case in much fine assembly work.

"Inspection" (10) is a function that may be handled by any one of the senses, and in fact is handled by the eye, the ear, the touch, the taste and the smell in many existing occupations of the present day. This, alone, is a help in the assignment of work, since it is an accepted theory that when one sense has become dulled, the others become sharpened, either through some compensation or through a greater amount of exercise. "Transport, loaded" (6), "Position for next operation" (11), "Release load" (12), these all are in many cases taken care of through gravity, or through some mechanical means of conveyance. "Transport Empty" (13), which means carrying the working member back to the place of beginning work, may be controlled so that it uses the least amount of effort and results in the least amount of fatigue possible. Laboratory investigations have proved that there is a tendency for the empty hand to return to the work-place through a higher path than is used when the hand is loaded, this doubtless being caused by the release from tension and a natural inclination to spring up into the air without realizing the ultimate fatigue from lifting the weight unnecessarily through the higher arc. Pre-arrangement of the material, or simply calling attention to the fact, may do much to cut down this unnecessary fatigue. "Waiting (for avoidable delay," 14), can be utilized for "Rest" (16). "Waiting (for avoidable delay," 15) can be immediately eliminated, through a proper study of the operation. In this way we have again a combination of two or three elements. No individual operation need cover all these sixteen elements. Some may cover many less; a large number, during the present imperfect state of development of efficiency in most operations, have an element repeated many times. The fact remains that this method of studying an operation will immediately result, not only in calling attention to possible improvements, but also in showing opportunities for cripples to enter the work. This has been called the motion study method of attack, and in actual practice has proved itself most efficient.

There can be little doubt as to the efficiency of these various methods for finding opportunities for the cripples in present-day industrial work. There must, however, be a question as to what will happen to the workers already in these positions, and what changes must be made in our relations with labor and in present-day classifications of the trades. Undoubtedly during war conditions many of these opportunities will present themselves automatically, as the younger men are transferred into active service and the men of larger experience are transferred or promoted to more complicated work. The entrance of women and of cripples into many trades now considered necessarily done by unmaimed men workers is already an existing condition in the industrial world. It remains rather to consider whether the returning cripples shall be welcomed in the industries and placed at the most fitting occupations with the least delay possible, or shall be allowed to enter as a matter of necessity on a competitive basis, and be placed at occupations which are not fitted for them, and shifted from place to place until the adjustment shall take place. Those who are acquainted with the psychological aspect of the problem and who know how much the cripples need encouragement and the feeling that they are welcomed back into all social activities of the community, can realize the importance of deciding this question at once. It is simply facing a necessary solution of the problem and providing that it shall take place with the largest benefits possible to all elements concerned. The industries *must* take the cripples. The cripples *must* be put at work. The only matter open for decision now is how efficiently and with how much satisfaction to the cripples this adjustment can take place.

As for the necessary classification of the trades, this is a matter that was pending long before the war.[1] Those who have been interested in trade development and have made studies of the problems involved throughout the last 20 years must realize that reclassification of the trades is basic if this country is to attain and hold her fitting place in the world's trade.[2] Here again we have not a decision to make as to what will come, but simply as to how we will bring the necessary results about in the best method possible. The trades are, at this very time, being reclassified in order to allow the women and the cripples to come in to do that work which they are capable of doing, to the advantage of the work and to themselves, and this condition cannot and will not cease when the war closes. Because of fixed physical limitations, the cripple will have to turn out a certain amount of product of a certain fixed quality. Because of humanitarian conditions, he must work in an environment where all unnecessary fatigue is eliminated, and where rest from necessary fatigue is provided. The same holds true with the introduction of women into the industries, where they have not formerly been. Unless proper provision for fatigue elimination is made, disastrous

---

[1] "Motion Study," 94. New York, D. Van Nostrand Co., 1911.

[2] "Applied Motion Study," Chapter I. New York, MacMillan Co., 1917.

results will inevitably follow,[1] and have already followed where restrictions have been done away with even temporarily.[2] Again, the question of proper selection, placement and promotion are vital at this time.[3] As has been said, "We are involved not only in the task of winning the war but of *winning the peace.*" If we are to do this latter we must provide for the new elements entering into our industries; for all practical purposes the cripple is a new element, being an entirely different man in many respects than the man who went out of the trade.

We must provide for the least amount of waste possible in the handling of this human element. A solution along these lines lies in a new form of education, that is, in teaching the one best way according

---

[1] "Industrial Liberty in War Time." An Address by Sect. of War Newton D. Baker before the Consumers' League at Baltimore, November 14, 1917.

[2] "Industrial Fatigue and Its Relation to Maximum Output," by Henry J. Spooner, London Polytechnic. Co-Partnership Publishers, Ltd., London, England. Reprinted from *Co-Partnership* (December, 1916—May, 1917).

Also, "Industrial Fatigue and Its Causes," by Prof. A. Stanley Kent of the University of Bristol, England. A Series of Reports published by Darling & Sons, Ltd., London, England.

Also, "Industrial Efficiency and Fatigue in British Munition Factories." U.S. Dept. of Labor, Bureau of Labor Statistics, *Bulletin No.* 230.

[3] "Adequate Promotion as a Solution of the Labor Turnover Problem," a paper presented before the Brooklyn Institute of Arts and Sciences, February, 1918.

to which an activity is to be done.[1] This teaching and its results will automatically provide workers whom it is easy to select, to place and to promote.

Again, the question of monotony, so much discussed and so little understood, must be faced immediately. Monotony is not the result of repeating the same operation according to the same method a great number of times.[2] It is the result of doing work which does not occupy the attention, and, because of having nothing to hold the interest and attention, allowing the mind to follow the manual operation in an endless, tiring, deadening sequence. The remedy for monotony consists of two things. First, reducing all possible elements of the operation to an efficient habit,[3] thus giving to the mind freedom from unnecessary repetitive decisions, and second, making the work so interesting, through motion study and fatigue study, and through enlisting the coöperation of the workers, that it becomes a stimulating exercise. This is possible, is practical, and *has already been done* to the distinct advantage of both work and worker.

---

[1] "The Place of the Educator in the New Education." American Association for the Advancement of Science (1917), Sec. L.

[2] "Applied Motion Study," Chapter VIII, 158.

[3] "Psychology of Management," 234. New York, MacMillan Co., 1914.

As to the attitude of organized labor to the admission of crippled soldiers into the industries, we cannot but believe that the Unions will be prompt to welcome the " weaker brother " back into the ranks, and to coöperate in every way possible toward his most advantageous placement just as they have been glad to coöperate in other industrial war measures. The preliminary step toward having the employer and the union agree on this matter is for them to start immediately a campaign of agreement along lines where they already agree. For example, both employer and employee are vitally interested in fatigue study, and its results benefit both alike. Both employer and employee are interested in eliminating waste in order that the largest wages possible may be paid, and the greatest amount of contentment among employees may result. Undoubtedly, when such things as fatigue elimination have been agreed upon, the agreement as to the placement of the crippled soldier will come naturally. It must not be forgotten that the crippled soldier is only a specialized case of the industrial cripple returning to the industry. The latter is first an industrial worker, then a soldier, then a cripple, then again an industrial worker. The military experience may add to the capability or the initiative, and thus make the war cripple slightly different from the peace cripple, but if methods which prove successful in handling industrial cripples be applied to the war cripple no great errors will result. There is one thing besides to be considered ; namely, that the war cripple has probably passed through a more awful shock, therefore the period of readjustment should be made the simpler and easier.

We believe, then, that the problem of the crippled soldier in the industries can be most quickly and most profitably solved by considering it a variation of the problem of the industrial cripple, by teaching the returned soldier the particular work at which he can be most satisfied and most profitable, and by affording opportunities in the industries, through the coöperation of those in the industries, both employers and workers alike. We further believe that it is an important duty of the engiueer not only to see that the one best way is taught to the returning cripples, but that the one best opportunity is found for them in the industries.

Discussion

Bradley Stoughton, New York, N. Y.—In one way, I am sorry to speak first, because perhaps by speaking of the blind worker I shall turn aside the thoughts Major Gilbreth has so well presented, because we have blind men with us always, but we are going to have more crippled men than we have ever had before, and worse crippled men. I have been in blind work for a good many years and am much interested in our Association here in New York and have visited a good many other Associations in different parts of the country. When a blind man first knows of his affliction, he becomes most abnormally depressed. There is no sort of handicap or crippling that depresses a man at first so terribly as blindness. Generally for a month, sometimes for 2 months or 3 months, a man who is blind or who knows he is going blind wants to kill himself. In the first place, he does not want to live, and in the second place, he does not want to be a burden on his family. We have found, however, after more than 20 years' work, that if we can get a man over the first 2 months, we can generally make him a very valuable citizen. After that period, blind men are almost always the happiest of cripples. If any of you doubt it for a moment, I will get up a special excursion to our blind shop here in New York where we have nearly a hundred men doing different kinds of industrial work and you will find them singing and cracking jokes with one another and you will find them altogether a happy lot of men; but if you go to a deaf and dumb asylum, for example, you will find on the contrary that they are not happy and they get more unhappy all the time. That is the particular message I want to spread to everybody, because we are going to have a great many blind soldiers. Now, blinded men can do many useful things. Most of them, I regret to say, are manual rather than intellectual. Most of our laboring men make brooms; many of them make baskets; many of them cane chairs. If they are of a musical turn, they can tune pianos. Almost all of them are splendid masseurs. They are most excellent telepone operators and so on. The reason for it all is that blindness brings an extraordinary concentration and for telepone operating, for example, there is no distraction that makes you forget the number or forget to call up the number that was busy before, or many of those annoying things. It is the same way with stenography. A blind man can work one of these stenographic machines just as well as one who sees. It presses a little impression in the paper, he can draw that through his fingers and then type it on the typewriter. Now I want you to know of those things. I want you to tell everybody those things, that the information may go out and catch one or two men, so that if they become blinded in battle, they are going to think of it. I want to join with Major Gilbreth in asking every engineer and every manager present to bear in mind all the time how they can use crippled men, including blinded men.

L. D. HUNTOON, New York, N. Y.—I received a letter from the American Committee of Engineers in London in regard to preparing for the crippled soldiers. I immediately sent a copy of this letter to the fifteen directors of the Mining and Metallurgical Society, asking for suggestions and recommendations, and in that way I got in touch with Major Gilbreth. There is one letter here from one of our members, Stanly Easton, which I want to read.

"I have your letter enclosing copy of letter from the Chairman of the Sub-Committee on Crippled Soldiers, London, and in response to your invitation I have the following suggestion to offer: crippled soldiers should go back into industrial life and be put on an earning, if not a self-supporting, basis as quickly as possible, as much for their own good as for economic reasons. Having had some experience in handling men crippled in mining and affiliated work, I know that their mental and physical healing is hastened by following some interesting and gainful occupation rather than by loafing about, thinking of their misfortunes and listening to the condolences of their friends, even if they are receiving the best of care and comfort. I have found that there is some useful work for almost any crippled soldier, although I have never had a totally blind unfortunate victim to place. I have observed repeatedly that the victim of some accident, who has been very badly mutilated and who is desperately blue and discouraged, recovered his spirits and faced the future cheerfully just as soon as he got something to do that he could successfully handle. I believe the suggestion that men crippled in the National service be not discharged but kept in the army for at least a year is an excellent one, but they should be encouraged to take up their work where they left off in entering the service. With some strong and public-spirited organization, it is probable that such former employer can find something for them to do that will suit their impaired physical condition, particularly if some governmental or other influence is brought to bear on such employer and the military pay continued while the man is breaking into his new work. Young men, of whom our military forces are nearly entirely composed, develop rapidly along new lines when their old work is made impossible because of physical disability. I have noticed individuals who have never done any clerical or mental work gain very rapidly in this direction when an injury prevents them from continuing the manual labor which heretofore was their sole calling. Briefly my suggestion is, help these men get back into civilian life and take up their old work, or similar work, where they left it off, through the coöperation of their former employers and the government or some organization formed for such mission."

J. M. Glenn, New York, N. Y.—I desire to call attention to a paper issued by the Committee on Blindness. It is a very interesting study and can be had from the Committee on the Prevention of Blindness, which has its office in the Russell Sage Foundation Building, if anybody would like to get hold of it. It contains very valuable suggestions as to preventing blindness by accident and can be had from the Committee.

W. M. Kreglow, Palmerton, Pa.—In one instance that I can recall, a railroad man lost his leg; he has been trained since that as a machinist, and makes a better living after his injury than before. In one of our departments, the foreman at first said he could not place any cripples, but after analyzing the jobs we found that in 20 per cent. of them cripples could do the work.

C. R. Hook, Middletown, Ohio.—The men of our plant, the superintendents in the several departments, are really giving this matter serious consideration. Especially is that true of our chief surgeon and director of employment, who has had several conferences with me on this particular subject, and we have already started to study the different positions in the plant to discover those positions into which men who are totally disabled in one or more limbs, or partially impaired, can be put. To be specific, since railroad men have been mentioned, we had a man who was a conductor of one of the freight crews, who had his foot run over and the lower part of it taken off. He had had experience as a fireman at one time and was pretty thoroughly familiar with the work of the engineer. We put him back into the cab for a couple of weeks and let him work for the engineer and then we gave him a position as an engineer and he made more money as a locomotive engineer than he did as a conductor on the ground. We also have found places in our open-hearth plant, in our blooming mill and our bar mill department for men who have been disabled, by placing them as pulpit operators where the operator can sit up on a platform and operate levers that run the rolls, this way and that way, and shift guards this way and that way, or turn over a device or whatever it may be. He has got to be close enough to these levers to operate them. He can sit on a stool and operate the lever just as well as the fellow who has both his legs. In the open-hearth department, we have found places for men who have been crippled in various ways, by putting them in as door lifters. They operate the hydraulic and also the electrical apparatus which lifts the doors of the furnace; and there are several things of that kind around the plant which we have already discovered.

E. E. BACH, Ellsworth, Pa.—One man who worked in our mines lost his leg and we trained him for a stationary engineer; he didn't lose much earning power in the transition.

MARTIN L. GRIFFIN, Rumford, Maine.—We have to look at this matter through different eyes. There is no question about it that a cripple is not the most efficient man; he has lost a valuable asset, and we have to take into account that he has been defending his country, he has been defending our civilization, our homes and our rights, and we have no right whatever to draw the same lines that we would at other times. We are obligated to take care of him, and, as the gentleman has said here, there are a great many jobs that men who have lost some of their personal assets can fill. We have more accidents in our line of business than we wish we had, after complying with all the requirements of the law. Some of our men will, at times, lose their hands or their arms, but we always find employment for them. There is no question whatever that employment can be found for the soldier boys when they come back crippled, but, we shall have to change our viewpoint; we cannot select in the same way that we did before.

FIRST STEPS IN THE SOLUTION OF THE PROBLEM OF CRIPPLED SOLDIERS [1]

THE problem of the Crippled Soldiers stands before us demanding not only an immediate solution, but one that shall be of permanent value to the cripples and to the community of which they form a part. No delay is excusable, no half-way methods can be accepted, and a satisfactory solution demands not only a unified community willing to apply scientific methods but a change in attitude toward many existing activities.

There must be a great change in the general attitude of mind toward at least ten subjects of universal interest, and a refusal to accept any conclusions that are not the result of measurement. *First,* toward so-called "efficiency." At the beginning of the efficiency movement there was great admiration expressed not only for the ideals therein involved but for the practice into which these ideals formulated. Lately there has come a fashion of

[1] Presented at the Joint National Conference of the Western Efficiency Society and the Society of Industrial Engineers, Chicago, Ill., March 27-29, 1918.

confusing efficiency with ruthlessness, with lack of art, or with " dry as dust " methods. Now it must not be forgotten that real efficiency consists simply of attaining the desired end with the least expenditure of effort possible. What that end may be is determined by ethics. It must be said, however, that the aim of efficiency both in the industries and out is usually understood to be durable satisfaction and happiness both to the individual and to the social community involved. With this thought in mind any effort to decry efficiency and to confuse it with other terms and to think of it as anything but a synonym for waste elimination, for utilization and for valuable achievements, must be condemned if we are to get anywhere in solving such problems as that of the Crippled Soldier.

Second, an attitude of mind toward applied science must be changed, *i.e.*, the attitude that exists in the mind of many recent college graduates, unfortunately a preponderant number of them being women, that any science that has a practical end or is applied in a practical field thereby ceases to be " pure " and is not of the highest value. We must come to realize that thru applied science has come not only advances in the sciences working with material, but also in the human sciences, such as psychology. It has been applied science that has brought people in the industries to realize what actual measurement will do for them, and it is absolutely necessary that the thinkers of the world evaluate applied science properly if it is to accomplish its great work.

Third, the attitude toward " dignity of labor " must be changed. In theory the American people believe that any labor that is performed efficiently is dignified. In practice the same type that belittles applied science, belittles also anything but mental labor. The curriculum of the average college, the lack of training for the industries, the scorn of vocational guidance by those who are interested in so-called " cultural subjects " only, not only cuts off a large element of the community from such training as will result in ability to think and act in efficient motions, but also cuts off those who have been forced to content themselves with manual activity from a chance for that education that would insure all parts of the brain developing concurrently with those parts that develop accompanying the manual labor.

Fourth, there must be a change in attitude toward the necessity for reclassifying the trades. It has too long been thought that because in ancient times certain activities were considered as constituting a trade group there was something of Divine Right in this grouping which must be maintained. We are coming to realize, thru careful scientific investigations, and thru accumulating data that show the likenesses between various trades, that the division marks between them are poorly placed.[1] As women and cripples come into the trades it will become necessary to reclassify them from the standpoint of the type of thinking, of the manual skill demanded, etc. We must, therefore, if we wish to aid progress, come to accept the necessity for a reclassification of the trades and come to demand that this shall be based on the results of actual laboratory measurements, and upon these only.

Fifth, there must be a general change of attitude of mind toward cripples. It is absolutely undeniable that the average man and woman alike has felt that the cripple, thru his maiming, became a different sort of member of the community, to be shielded and pitied perhaps, but scarcely to be welcomed back into the activities of life. Again, women have been largely to blame here, and this feeling must entirely change if the cripple is to be made, as he must be made, a productive member of the community, with a share in social as well as in industrial life.[2] The shameful neglect of industrial cripples in this country

---

[1] See "Motion Study," D. Van Nostrand, 25 Park Place, New York City.

[2] See "Measurement of the Human Factor in Industry." Presented before the Western Efficiency Society, National Conference, May, 1917.

goes to prove what has been said. It is not the Labor Unions, with their well-known sympathy for the "weaker brother" who have been the prime movers, as Unions, in keeping the industrial cripples from coming back into the trades. It is the general feeling of individuals, as employers and employees alike, that the thought of a cripple re-entering competitive industrial life is repellent, that these people should be provided for by pensions in their homes. Through the new Crippled Soldier Work, where all cripples have been invited to give their histories and to contribute their experiences for the encouragement of the crippled soldiers, *for the first time* the cripples have been made to feel that they are an essential part of the community and that there is a call for what they can do.

In the *sixth* place there must be a different feeling toward industrial accidents. These have been in the past thought of as sad and calamitous but scarcely as criminal, which in many cases they are. The crippled-soldier problem, with the great number of men who inevitably are returning in a maimed condition, brings out clearly the shame and the crime of allowing men to be maimed in the peaceful pursuits of the industries. A strong emphasis on the seriousness of industrial accidents will be a great aid toward World Peace ultimately.

Seventh, there must be a general change in attitude of mind toward the Consumers League [1] and other allied activities that are aiming to supplement the work of the National Safety Council and other accident-preventing agencies by assuring to workers proper working conditions and hours. Those who wish to go into such work as the Crippled Soldier Work must first be sure that they are utilizing all existing activities which can contribute toward the cause. Otherwise we shall have a reduplication of effort, which in the present critical condition of our National affairs is little short of scandalous.

Eighth, there must be a general change of attitude of mind toward fatigue. Serious as accidents of all kinds are, the loss to the country is by no means so large as is the loss thru preventable, unnecessary fatigue. The whole subject of fatigue must come before the public mind and each and every one of us must determine that we will be instrumental in eliminating unnecessary fatigue and in providing rest for necessary fatigue before we can have done our share toward solving the new problem.[2]

Ninth, there must be a general change in the

---

[1] See "Industrial Liberty in Wartime," by Secretary of War Newton D. Baker. Delivered before the Consumers League, Baltimore, November, 1917.

[2] See "Fatigue Study." Macmillan Co., 5th Avenue, New York; George Routledge and Sons, Ltd., London.

attitude of mind toward the position of women in industry, and particularly of those women who are coming into industries usually performed by men, many of them women who have never been in the industries before. The Canadian women have taught the world a splendid lesson by their attitude, which doubtless was also shared by the English women. In every case they signified a desire to *supplement* the work of the men rather than to supplant them, as is splendidly brought out by Mrs. Harry Heustis, first woman superintendent of the munition workers in the Ross Rifle Factory at Quebec.[1]

Coming in with this attitude, they slipped into their assigned positions with the least amount of friction possible, and the adjustment became easy of accomplishment. This same attitude must be held by women, and must be held by the men of the country toward the women, *i.e.*, that the women are coming in to do what is best for every one that they shall do, and in a coöperative spirit, or we can get nowhere.

Tenth and finally there must be a general change of attitude toward motion economy. It must be realized that all activities, consisting as they do of motions and of decisions, consume a certain amount

[1] See Article by Mrs. Heustis in *Scientific American* of January 12, 1918.

of physical and concurrent mental activities; therefore, motion economy, performing an activity according to the best method and with the greatest amount of speed that it is possible to attain and at the same time not accumulate unnecessary or over-fatigue, is a National Duty.[1]

With these ten changes of attitude in mind, and the fundamental character that they must have, understood, we may turn, second, to the divisions of the Crippled Soldier Problem. We come at once to the problem of "first aid." The physical first aid is well understood and the need for immediate and constant, careful nursing. It is perhaps not so well understood that there is a concurrent psychological need, that the Crippled Soldiers demand from the first moment encouragement and accounts of those who have had similar experience and what they have been able to accomplish through the training and through the placement that is to become available. Along with this, or following shortly after, comes the necessity for early teaching. It is too late to wait till the crippled soldier returns to his home, it is too late to wait till he comes to this country, it is often too late to wait till he is in the camp. On his sick bed he must have the first mental and muscular training, if the re-education is to be as profitable as

[1] See "Fatigue Study."

possible, and if he is to have the greatest use of the maimed member. Next on the list comes the need for psychotherapy, the more scientific re-education outlined so well by Mr. George Edward Barton of Consolation House, Cliften Springs, New York, in his little book on " Re-Education." The whole process must be conducted with the least amount of waste possible, considering the man's physical and psychological condition, his past experience, the training that is available and the ultimate opportunity that he is to have.

These first aids having been considered, we turn now to the training of the Crippled Soldier, and consider first the teaching. The teachers of the Crippled Soldiers in the past have too often been simply such teachers as were available, who taught not what the cripple needed but what they themselves knew best.[1] As the result many a strong, hardy man became a weaver of baskets, a maker of toys, or a worker at some other feminine occupation. Now not only does the cripple himself crave to be back in the world of men and of actual production but also economic conditions demand that he be there. It is, therefore, our duty to provide immediately that fittingly trained teachers be available.

---

[1] See " The Engineer, the Cripple and the New Education." Presented before the A. S. M. E., December, 1917.

For this, of course, the next thing is money, and anyone who doubts his or her power to be of use in this problem can immediately be of great service, and learn more about the activities in the meantime, while collecting money for the cause. This the Red Cross Institute is already doing, supplementing thereby their work of collecting bibliographies, making studies of appliances, etc. The Association of Collegiate Alumni have undertaken to do a part of this work and the Red Cross Institute will welcome all other workers as individuals or in groups. Besides the teachers and the money there comes the need for utilization of existing activities. Here again much is being done. The staff of Teachers' College of Columbia University connected with the nursing have co-operated with the New York Infirmaries, in order that teachers may be trained in the re-education of its cripples and at the same time that the present industrial cripples may profit by the care and attention. In this way not only are existing opportunities utilized but the training furnished benefits all concerned.

The next point to be considered is the need for preparing opportunities for these cripples when they have been properly trained. These may be of three sorts; *first*, new opportunities, that is discovery of work that needs to be done but has never been properly covered. As an example of this we may consider the occupation of the Dental Nurse, which is coming into existence in certain states and is being strenuously opposed in others. This work consists of taking from the already overcrowded work of the dentist, the work simply of keeping the teeth cleaned, and assigning this to a properly trained, certificated and inspected nurse. Through laboratory study we have discovered that this work may be satisfactorily done by a one-eyed, one-armed, legless cripple. The *second* type of opportunity is that of the "set-aside" occupation, which will be satisfactory for a cripple and which does not demand the capabilities of the whole man or woman. Such would be the running of a small store, the tending of a telephone, the running of cash register, etc. Again, thru laboratory experiments, we have demonstrated the possibilities of these occupations proving profitable. The *third* type of opportunity is that where the cripple is placed on a competitive basis with whole workers. This may be brought about in two ways, first, through artificial limbs or attachments. This we have called the Amar Method because of the wonderful work along this line done by Prof. Jules Amar of Paris. Second, through appliances fastened to the cripple or through changes in existing apparatus or machinery. Such has been the work in this country. For example, work with typists where, through attachments of multiple rolls and the use of ribbons instead of carbons, it is possible for a one-armed man to compete satisfactorily on short letters with a two-armed typist working according to present-day methods, and the second example that of magnetized hammer and rocking box which enables a one-armed man to accomplish nailing with as much speed and exactitude as can a two-armed man with the ordinary apparatus. This method is peculiarly fitted to the American type of mind, which delights in invention.

Perhaps the most important thing in the whole problem, the most significant, is the necessity for combining heart and brain in whatever work is done, the heart for the sympathy to provide the incentive. If we lose this attitude of pity, which has been the attitude toward the cripple of the past, we certainly lose our chief incentive to enter into the Crippled Soldier Work. No desire for a better economic condition, no passion for a new type of education, *nothing* can take the place of the warm human sympathy that sends one into the Crippled Soldier Work, and makes him ready and glad to welcome the returned cripple and to help him to the best of his ability. But this "heart" work by itself can accomplish little, and what is accomplished often has to be undone or done over. Along with this must come the brain work. Here arises the necessity of first discovering the *one best way*. Too long have we been satisfied, as educators and as people, to teach the *available* way and to allow the learner to come to some decision, by himself, as to what is the best way. A study of habit and of habit interference shows that we have here a most wasteful process. The learner vacillates from one method to another, and, if he is of a decisive type, often comes to a method which is not highly efficient. If he does come to an efficient method, he seldom really knows why it is efficient, and whether he is right in keeping to it or not. Under the new education the *one best way* will be discovered according to laboratory methods. That and that only will be taught, and the learner will be forced to perform activity in that way until he understands it thoroughly. Then a suggestion will be in order, and will be carefully tested and incorporated, that the learner of the next generation may progress from the highest point that we have succeeded in reaching.[1]

Accompanying the *one best way* will be the effective transference of skill: the knowledge that what one man has must be passed on to the others

---

[1] See "Psychology of Management." The Macmillan Co., New York.

who need it, in the most efficient method possible. The learning process must be simplified by the fact that both teacher and pupil are trained for their functions, and that both know that what they are doing is for the ultimate and immediate good of themselves and the world. And with these two comes the attitude of mind that is fixed constantly on making measurements and on abiding by the results of measurement. There is a feeling, and has always been, that measurement is inartistic, that "hit-or-miss" is more beautiful, more stimulating, more satisfying. Yet all the great works of art conform absolutely to measurement, the great pictures, the great statues, the great symphonies, all make their appeals because they fulfill a fundamental human desire for accuracy. Expertness, skill is satisfying wherever it is found—in the sports, in the industries, in the professions. No matter what the work may be, where *skill*, where *accuracy* exists, where measurement is recognized, there we have smoothness, grace, beauty and satisfaction.

To solve the Crippled Soldier Problem, then, we must have a general change in the attitude of mind, a recognition of the fundamental necessities of the Crippled Soldier Problem, and the desire to enter into the solution not only with our hearts, but with our minds also. It is a big problem. Perhaps there is none more pressing facing the world to-day. Upon its solution will depend not only the possibilities of winning the war, but those far greater possibilities involved in Winning the Peace.

MOTION STUDY FOR THE BLINDED: A METHOD OF MAKING THE HANDICAPPED MODELS OF INDUSTRIAL EFFICIENCY

MOTION STUDY for the blinded, like Motion Study for the crippled, involves three branches of work—teaching the teachers of the blinded, teaching the blinded themselves, and discovering opportunities in the industries where the taught can be satisfactorily placed.

The teachers of the blinded must be convinced at the outset that their aim in the past—namely, to teach the blind to do certain things as well as they were done by the sighted—was wrong. The methods ordinarily in use by the sighted are far from efficient. The teachers of the blinded must realize this, and must recognize the fact that the blinded must be taught NOT *the method ordinarily in use but the One Best Way of performing each selected activity.* When this is generally understood and practised not only will the efficiency of the blinded workers be greatly increased, but also they will serve as *models to the sighted*, to the benefit of all concerned. Having realized the necessity of teaching the One Best Way, it will be necessary for the teachers of the blinded then to acquire this One Best Way themselves, thru intensive Motion Study; to reconsider the activities that they have been in the habit of transferring to the blinded from the standpoint of Motion Economy and Fatigue Elimination; to make themselves familiar with the findings of scientific investigations and industrial practice in these activities, and to incorporate the results of their investigations into a most efficient teaching and learning process. Up to this point the training of teachers of the blinded is exactly similar to that of others preparing themselves to teach different groups. What this training should be and how it should be given, we have endeavored to set forth in "Motion Study," "Fatigue Study" and "Applied Motion Study," and have presented the reasons for giving such training in "The Psychology of Management."

There are certain points, however, important in all teaching that must be strongly emphasized in the teaching of the blind. The first of these is *the importance of instilling at the outset habits of right motions.* Not only will forming such habits enable the blinded to accomplish the desired end in the shortest possible amount of time, but also it will prevent that interference of wrong habit which is especially serious for this type of worker. The eyes serve as an admirable inspection and corrective

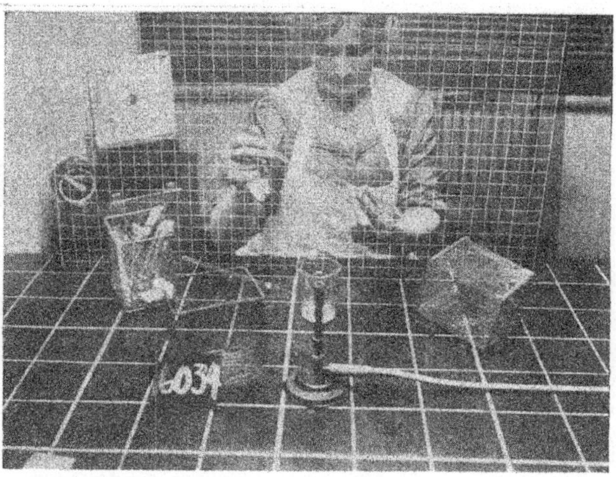

THE "PENETRATING SCREEN" FOR RECORDING THE MOTIONS OF THE "ONE BEST WAY" OF PERFORMING AN OPERATION

The vast difference in efficiency of the usual way, as compared with the One Best Way, is so important that it is advisable to record in great detail the methods of the most expert operator performing the work in the best manner known.

[*face p.* 148

WIRE MODELS OF THE PATHS OF MOTIONS

For enabling blind and also sighted workers to "visualize" the One Best Way to do work. One of the most important pieces of knowledge to teach all workers is to think in terms of elements of motions, and there is no one thing that will help so efficiently to teach this as will a motion model.

This particular collection of motion models is in the Smithsonian Institute, Washington, D.C. For wire models of progress of learning of best motions see *Applied Motion Study*, Fig. 16, p. 90.

device for the sighted worker when trying to overcome a wrong habit. Lacking their aid, the blinded worker must make a greater struggle to overcome wrong habit interference, and to bring the work—and what is more important, the method of performing the work—back to standard.

The second point to be stressed is the necessity of the *elimination of all unnecessary fatigue.* The general condition of fatigue carelessness, not to say fatigue ignorance, in all countries is shocking, among the blinded as among the sighted. The average desk and chair given to blind workers could hardly be designed to cause more fatigue. Perhaps because of his handicap, the blinded worker is apt to remain contented when trained to a satisfying activity. It is, therefore, from all standpoints, necessary and economical that he be provided *from the outset* with the most scientifically deviced fatigue elimination devices, not only that he may accomplish the most output with the least amount of effort, but also that they may assist him toward forming habits which will be finally, as well as at the outset, most efficient. The necessity of eliminating unnecessary fatigue must also be held in mind when choosing those trades or activities for which the blinded are to be trained. We go so far as to say not only that trades which do not cause a large amount of fatigue should be chosen for the blinded, but also that many of them might profitably be trained for the specialized work of eliminating unnecessary fatigue in the industries and serve as examples of what can be done along such lines.

A third point to be emphasized is the *close relationship between efficient habits and automaticity,* and the benefits of rendering all possible activities automatic. The blinded have themselves illustrated this point marvellously, thru their success with typing. All typing schools recognize the fact that the practice of striking the keys without looking at them will give the best results. Here, of course, the blinded have the advantage, as they have not even to struggle against the desire to look at the keys. Many typing schools for the blinded and the sighted recognize that striking a certain key with a certain finger is good practice, but very few recognize the effect upon automaticity resulting from *never* striking a key with any other than the standard finger. *It is the " exception to the rule " that postpones automaticity. It is the automaticity that permits high output without the monotony of superattention on unimportant repetitive decisions.* These conclusions are the results of many experiments in Motion Study in our laboratory, and we cannot over-emphasize their importance in effecting ultimate skill and in shortening the time

THE ROUTE MODEL

By means of this and similar devices the standard locations and paths of least waste can be "visualized" by the blind by the sense of touch.

Route models are necessary for the sighted to understand relative locations and standard paths properly, and they can also be used with similar success by the blind.

These route models are made to scale, and the locations of workplaces, offices, rest rooms, store rooms, and paths for least waste can be represented by strings of different size and texture.

The different kinds of workers can be represented by different kinds of tacks.

[*face p.* 150

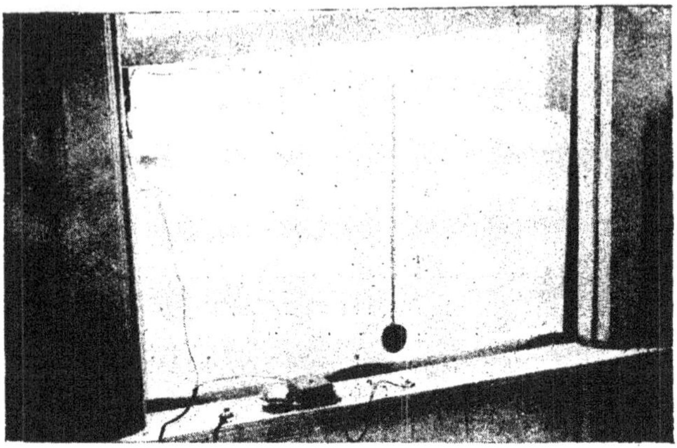

TIMING DEVICE FOR DEAF OR BLIND

Each oscillation of the pendulum flashes the light and also rings the bell. This device has been used where short periods of time must be known on work requiring the entire attention.

[*face p.* 151

of the learning period. We not only believe the blinded have achieved wonderful results in typing, but that in many cases the teaching of the sighted would be improved if the teachers would adopt the methods that have proved successful in training the blinded.

While the *method* of teaching has thus been successful, there is much to be criticised in the *material* used. Following out the theory of achieving super-automaticity with least practice, we recommend concentrating on sentences containing words used most frequently in correspondence. For example, such sentences as "It is the will of all that you and I go into it for a good prize" furnish typical examples of sentences containing words used very often. In fact, fifteen of the eighteen words used in this sentence will average 30 per cent of the words written in American business correspondence. The following fifty words taken from Dr. Leonard Ayars' book "Measurement of Ability in Spelling" show the words commonest in American business correspondence and form a list representing almost 50 per cent. of the words in the order of their frequency.

the	it	at	dear	has
and	was	we	from	very
of	is	on	are	were
to	will	he	all	been

a	have	but	so	she
in	not	my	one	or
that	with	this	if	there
you	be	his	they	her
for	your	which	had	an

This list of words arranged into sentences will help to get *super-skill with least practice.* Such sentences as the following by John Fox, a pupil at the Illinois School for the Blind, Jacksonville, Illinois: "My dear friend, we have been given fifty words and were told that whoever was clever enough to form a sentence of all the words, and if he or she had his or her answer in on a certain date, they would receive a prize; so I thought that you, by using your brain, could help me with this work; but at best it will not be an easy task for us, as the list from which these words are taken is a difficult one to arrange properly and there has been very little time to do it," which won the prize we offered in a contest among the blind pupils of the Illinois School for the Blind, Jacksonville, Illinois, under the guidance of Mr. Robert Woolston, show how simple a matter it is to arrange the words into some sort of continuity, and thus furnish simple and available practice material. It is advisable that the blinded pupils invent these sentences for themselves, as in this way they memorize the words easily and become interested, thru personal contact, in the underlying principle. Note, however, that these words should be arranged in different sentences at frequent intervals, for we have already found that if the same sentence is written too often the automaticity of the combined motions will result in the student having a tendency to continue writing phrases of the practice sentence beyond the place where it is identical with unfamiliar copy.

A fourth point to be stressed is that *along with this instruction in automaticity must come a teaching as to the WHY* of every method presented. Such teaching not only prevents automaticity from causing monotony, but also provides opportunity for invention upward, and stimulates such invention. This teaching of the WHY divides itself into consideration of the decisions involved, which necessitates a training in elementary psychology and a study of the variables of Motion Study and of the elements of a motion. This apparently highly technical material is available and may be presented in such simple form that it will make any activity performed not only intelligible but also interesting.

A fifth point to be emphasized in teaching the blind is the *necessity of training in visualization.* The importance of this is being realized more and more thruout all training. In the case of executives visualization of facts as indicating tendencies or trends is achieved in many cases by presenting facts graphically on cross-sectioned paper. But it must not be forgotten that the entire science of graphical statistics is at the disposal of everyone, no matter what his training, capabilities or work, and that the usefulness of the science depends entirely upon the degree of skill with which it is adapted to the especial needs of the group or the individual using it. In the case of the blinded, from the very outset of the training use should be made of cross-sectioned devices for "locationing" tools, appliances, materials, etc. A cross-sectioned desk will show best to a worker how, thru standard "locationing," he can reduce the problems of the elements of "search," "find" and "select" of his various implements and tools to a minimum, and also get the speed that comes from the resulting automaticity. The same is true regarding "pre-positioning" of articles to be "grasped," "assembled" and "used." The problem of "find" can be simplified by placing the material of the right kind, in the right quantity, at the right place, at the right time. The problem of "select" is simplified by having material of slightly different quality always placed on different squares or groups of squares, whether it be on the bench, on the shelf in the storeroom or wherever the particular supply may be at any given time.

THE CROSS-SECTIONED VISUALIZING BOARD

By means of removable tacks and strings simultaneous motion cycle charts can be explained to, and thoroughly understood by, the blind. It is well to call attention to the fact that methods of least waste cannot be obtained nor properly taught without simultaneous motion cycle charts. No one thing can be done for the blind or for the sighted that will enable them to be so efficient as intensive teaching of motion study by means of these charts. The chart shown facing page 31 is that of the motions of changing paper in the typewriter of Miss Hortense Stollnitz, champion typist of the world, who was taught a method that enabled her to change her paper in a Remington typewriter in less than two seconds. The first picture shows the method of teaching the use of the Visualizing Board, and the second picture shows a listener following with the fingers an oral description of a simultaneous motion cycle chart.

[*face p. 15*

THE CROSS-SECTIONED VISUALIZING BOARD

The lecturer who is explaining a method of work will have no difficulty in having his ideas followed as clearly by the blind as though they could see his blackboard, if each is furnished with a Visualizing Board on which he can follow with his fingers the oral description. The "locationing" of tools, materials, and equipment on the bench or desk is of great importance for greatest automaticity and least waste of time and effort. Even the standardizing of the expected location on the table of the knife, fork, spoon, dishes, salt, and pepper will help him to proceed with least fumbling and conspicuousness.

[*face p.* 155

Let us take a simple example. Let the blind understand the location and relative position of the numbers on a cross-sectioned locationing board and he can be told instantly where he will find the various knives, forks, spoons, cups, saucers, salt, pepper, mustard, etc., that comprise his equipment at the dining-table. All that he needs is a little practice on the locationing board and he will be able to "visualize" the expected location of these things. The same thing is true in the industries. Besides its usefulness as a device for locationing material and simplifying motions, the visualizing board can be used as a device to accompany lectures and to enable the lecturer to present his subject more clearly. This visualizing board is marked in four-inch squares, and then again in inch squares, as is the visualizing board of the sighted; only instead of painted lines, the cross-sectioning is made by lines grooved into the background, and the numbers and letters, instead of being merely painted on the squares, are grooved in such a manner that they can be easily distinguished by touch. By the use of strings and pins, learning curves, charts, or drawings of any description can be reproduced. These the blind can follow with the finger during the progress of the lecture, and thus be enabled to visualize the subjects that the lecturer is describing. The use of such a device will make it profitable for the blind to listen to many lectures which have before this time been with difficulty understood, due to the lack of ability of speakers so to describe with words as to enable the blind to visualize the ideas embodied. All engineers, for example, are notorious for being unable to express or convey ideas without drawing or sketching while talking, and many others are dependent almost wholly upon the use of blackboards for conveying ideas. By means of the visualizing board it is possible for the ideas to be presented in graphical form so that the blinded can get the benefit of all the advances being constantly made in the method of presentation of facts.

The visualizing board is also used in connection with the motion model for teaching the theory of motions. Every blind student should be taught the theory of paths of motions and the effect of the variables of Motion Study upon the paths of motions. Each student should make a wire model of what he believes to be the path of some simple operation (*see* Figs. facing p. 20). The path of the left hand of a worker handling a sensitive drill is an ideal study, for one reason among many, that we have already many models of this particular example, and it is possible for the student to compare his results with those arrived at by experts. The chronocycle-

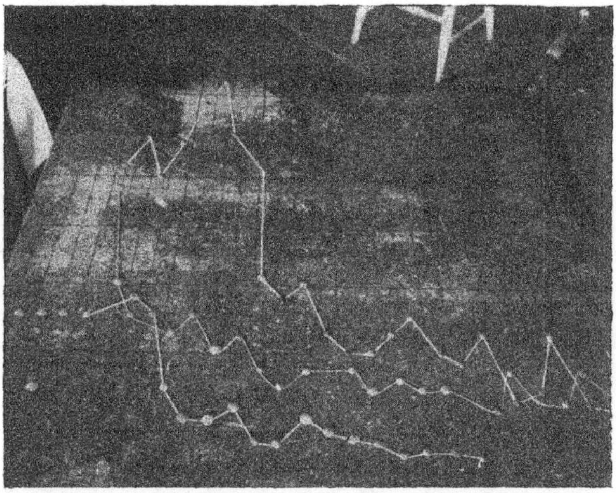

THE CROSS-SECTIONED VISUALIZING BOARD

By means of tacks and string, learning curves of three different workers are shown on the cross-sectioned Visualizing Board This device puts at the disposal of the blind the fund of information that otherwise would be, at best, difficult for them to obtain. Without knowledge of the effect upon learning curves of different methods of teaching, neither teacher nor pupil will be able to co-operate enthusiastically in the new pedagogical methods that take advantage of least habit interference, greatest automaticity, greatest skill with least practice, and importance of concentration on the One Best Way to do work.

MICROMOTION LABORATORY,

where opportunities for blinded workers are being investigated and methods of performing the work are being standardized.

[*face p.* 157

graph method of making records with a tuning-fork can be described either as a series of light spots or a series of sound spots, and the position and vibration of the arms of the tuning-fork can be quite easily visualized by touch. When the motion model has been made these light spots can be represented by strings wound around the wire, the tight coil representing the blunt end of the spark or intense end of the beginning of the flash of light or blast of sound, and the spaced coil representing the last or dying end of the light or sound. The fading out of the light or the loose end of the string represents the direction of the motion, just as the point of a bullet or shell in the air represents the direction in which the bullet or shell is travelling. Thru these adaptations of the motion models to make it respond more closely to the discriminations of the sense of touch and by placing the motion model upon the visualizing board, it is possible for the blinded student to come to an excellent understanding of the paths of motions and the elements therein involved. It is not until after one has made at least one model that one can appreciate that the motions involved determine the quantity and quality of the output and the resulting fatigue and monotony. The study of the wire model of any kind of work will prove incontestably that *there is no such thing as "unskilled work," but that there is everywhere an astounding amount of unskilled labor, in every activity.*

The sixth point to be emphasized is constantly demonstrating to the blinded, *his likenesses to rather than his differences from other people.* This the Motion Study Method of instruction will insure; for, as has been shown, the same devices and methods are used, with only such modifications as enable the blinded to accomplish the learning process more quickly. Along with this teaching the blinded are told that they are to be placed in the industries alongside of, often in competition with, and always in coöperation with, the sighted workers. This is made possible thru so functionalizing the work that such parts of it as keeping tools in condition are done by the sighted for the blind, while all parts of the work that can be done by the blinded are assigned to them.

The seventh point and final point to be emphasized is the fact that, especially in this stage of the work, *the blinded may act as models for the entire industrial world.* This is proving a great stimulus. If the point is emphasized early in the training and reiterated often, the blinded will feel that they are "set apart" only in such degree as they make themselves more efficient than their fellows, and are looked up to by them.

Along with the instruction of the teachers and of the blinded themselves goes a survey of industrial opportunities for those prepared to accept them. An excellent outline for such a survey is presented by Mr. A. B. Segur in "Industrial Management." The writers coöperated with Mr. Segur in gathering data of various industries. Three occupations were intensively studied, core-making for foundries, chair-making, and typing by the use of a typewriter and a dictaphone, and all were found admirably fitted to the blinded. The employment of totally blind workers in many kinds of core-making including many formerly considered impossible for blind workers, was found perfectly practicable, with satisfactory results to the employers and high wages to the blind operators, who could compete in this work without either charity or philanthropy. Core-making furnshes a large field of employment, as it is an industry confined to no one place, but to be found in all parts of the United States and other countries. It proved to be well adapted to even those blind who have had little schooling and who had neither been educated by the usual processes of the sighted nor by the special processes of the blind, as it required no knowledge of reading, writing, arithmetic, spelling or even measuring. It is one of the few inside trades where the worker cannot spoil or waste material during his period of least skill, at the beginning of his learning period. This makes it an especially desirable trade, as the employers themselves are more patient with the learners. The different kinds of core-making are so numerous as to furnish work for the different grades of mentality in the blind, and there is also sufficient variety to relieve monotony even in any one grade of work. This is very desirable, for while it is possible to render even a fundamentally monotonous type of work interesting by explanation of the psychology, physiology and minutiæ of motions involved, and by providing for frequent rest and recreational intervals, it is a natural advantage to have the work itself furnish interest. It also, in its highest and most complicated grades, furnishes ample opportunity for satisfying the yearnings of the most ambitious. Again, it furnishes requirements for all grades of muscular ability and strenuosity. Here it is to be commended as being a "real job"; the work of a producer; economically necessary, and therefore satisfying the economic sense of the worker who scorns to be a social parasite. As for possible costs, at the beginning undoubtedly some of the cores will be broken by the blind in the act of disassembling the core-boxes, but this can be avoided in some cases by

JOBS FOR THE BLIND

Motion Studies of the methods of the most expert moulders. This work was done for Lieutenant Colonel James E. Bordley of the Surgeon-General's Department, under the able supervision of Mr. A. B. Segur and Prof. L. W. Wallace. This is one of many studies made of different trades which have certain laws as to placement of blind workers, such as "if the laws of the division of labor are properly applied, and there is enough work to employ the handicapped worker continuously at one of the divisions of work that he can do, so as to use his complete strenuosity, he can earn the pay of an expert."

[*face p.* 160

CROSS-SECTIONED DESK FOR RECORDING THE BEST METHODS OF CHAMPIONS

After the best methods of champions have been recorded, as to time, space, and location of motions, they can be explained, taught, and practised by the sighted or blind workers. The difference between the efficiency of the best workers and the average workers is astounding, and to teach the method of the average worker is a shocking waste to those who know the difference.

[*face p.* 161

devising guides for guiding the motions of disassembly of the boxes. Collision of cores being placed on the core packets can be avoided by recording the occupied location of the cores on the packets by the location of the worker's feet on the foot-rest. Broken and imperfect cores can be sorted and thrown back into the said pile by an inspector with eyes. Every other possible objection to employment of the blind in this work can be overcome as simply as can this one. We found the manufacturers enthusiastic coöperators in this work, and anxious to afford all possible opportunities to our trained workers.

We also found many available opportunities for the employment of the blinded in the chair-making industry. Here were seen opportunities where one blind man might to advantage be added to an existing gang of two sighted men, and as a result the output of the machine and its two men could be doubled. This illustrates the possibility of relieving sighted workers of parts of their work that do not require sight, thus enabling them to devote their entire time to sighted work, and furnishing for the blinded interesting, profitable, remunerative employment. The chair-making industry furnishes an admirable field for functionalization of work, and, while some jobs undoubtedly cannot be fully completed by the blind, at the same time the full energy of a blind man can be utilized. *Any kind of work or any part of an operation that will utilize the full energy of a blind man will give him good earnings. Concentration on this thought is more important than pondering over the question of how to teach the blind to do the entire operation.*

We found that Mr. Segur had already obtained most admirable results in the work of the typist. He had already proved that a blind worker making use of a dictating-machine is able to compete successfully with a sighted stenographer-typist. In fact, if any office is large enough to employ also a sighted girl to make the corrections, a blind dictating-machine-typist can easily be much more efficient than a sighted stenographer-typist. A few simple improvements will make the operations more fit to be standardized. Thru a simple mechanism, a blind typist can be enabled to *hear the notations for corrections that are marked with pen or pencil upon the correction slip of the dictating machine, and to use sound for this notification as the sighted use sight.* We have also devised a counter to put on the mechanism operating the line spacer which is read able by touch at any line at any time, and this will also notify by sound at any desired line, thus overcoming the difficulty of locating any line or the position of the lower edge of the paper. We have also devised another use of the customary stylus of the blind for enabling them to locate the space for inserting paragraphs, or, instead of this, we may locate the places by standard indentations or holes thru the left-hand margin of the letter paper. If there is objection to minute indentations from 1/32 to 3/32 of an inch diameter in the paper, they can be pressed out by rubbing against a hard surface. These holes may be punched by the printer, or made to a template by the blind operator. Such devices are useful also for automatically locating the lower edge of the sheet, to make sure the paper is being utilized to its last line without stopping to investigate and feel the location of the lower edge of the paper, as is now common practice.

In order to enable the dictating-machine-typist to attain the greatest amount of efficiency, the dictator must also be taught to dictate properly. The dictator should at least say " paragraph " when he expects the typist to start a new paragraph, otherwise the typist may, and too often does, make a new sentence in the same paragraph that belongs to the next paragraph. Experience shows that the more fully the punctuation is dictated the more careful the composition. Therefore, this practice has advantages to the dictator as well as the transcriber. Again, to attain the greatest efficiency the standard desk and standard desk supplies demanded by the One Best Way should be used. These are especially adapted to blind workers. As the result of these, when two or more blind workers are in the same office their work places are interchangeable at all times.

The three typical occupations here described can be handled by workers who have either education, experience or good minds, or a combination of these three qualities. These occupations should be supplemented by others better fitted to those who are weak physically, where they can not only be made self-supporting but also prosperous. Such, for example, as the tending of small stores or booths or even mere counters with the addition of specially selected handwork to make productive their minutes of "unavoidable delay," such as during the time when there is no customer to whom to sell. As an example of scores of kinds of work that can be profitably used, let us cite the making of small picture frames in a mitre box requiring almost no time at all for "starting," "stopping" and "changing to and from" the work of attending the customer. Such supplementary occupations are easily to be found.

Work for the blinded is making most extraordinary progress, for the reason that it has been undertaken both in this country and abroad in the most liberal spirit and that it has enlisted the most widespread coöperation. All work being done is for all blinded, civilian as well as military. The findings in each country among the allied nations have been placed freely at the disposal of the others. Sir Arthur Pearson, Bart., the great leader whose remarkable work at St. Dunstan's is known thruout the world, has visited and inspected what is being done in this country, and experts from this side have visited and are being welcomed in England and on the Continent. Of all the handicapped the blinded have perhaps appealed most to the sympathy. It is, therefore, the more fitting that they should lead in the great task of demonstrating to the world what can be done *in spite of* a handicap and sometimes *because* of it.

The blind as a class have led the world in the "sport" of overcoming great handicap. Let us do our part for them, and, together with them, demonstrate to the sighted workers how to *achieve the One Best Way with the least unnecessary fatigue—the greatest of all problems in industrial reconstruction.*

THE END

Spotted something that isn't quite right?

Let us know and we'll fix it for future reprints. And as a thank you for your diligence, we'll send you a free Sothis book of your choice.

publisher@sothis.press

This page intentionally left blank

Except of course for that line above. And this one.
And whilst we have your attention, perhaps you'd
like to follow us on Instagram @sothis.press. Go on.

Made in the USA
Monee, IL
08 November 2026

68001563R00142